W0111538

▶ **Gizmos or: The Electronic Imperative**

DOI: 10.1057/9781137565457.0001

Also by Arthur Asa Berger

ADS, FADS & CONSUMER CULTURE (*2000*)

JEWISH JESTERS (*2001*)

THE MASS COMM MURDERS
Five Media Theorists Self Destruct (*2002*)

THE AGENT IN THE AGENCY (*2003*)

THE PORTABLE POSTMODERNIST (*2003*)

DURKHEIM IS DEAD
Sherlock Holmes Is Introduced to Social Theory (*2003*)

MEDIA AND SOCIETY (*2003*)

GAMES AND ACTIVITIES FOR MEDIA, COMMUNICATION AND CULTURAL
STUDIES STUDENTS (*2004*)

OCEAN TRAVEL AND CRUISING (*2004*)

DECONSTRUCTING TRAVEL
A Cultural Perspective (*2004*)

MAKING SENSE OF MEDIA
Key Texts in Media and Cultural Studies (*2004*)

SHOP TILL YOU DROP
Perspectives on American Consumer Culture (*2004*)

THE KABBALAH KILLINGS (*2004*)

VIETNAM TOURISM (*2005*)

MISTAKE IN IDENTITY
A Cultural Studies Murder Mystery (*2005*)

50 WAYS TO UNDERSTAND COMMUNICATION (*2006*)

THAILAND TOURISM (*2008*)

THE GOLDEN TRIANGLE (*2008*)

THE ACADEMIC WRITER'S TOOLKIT
A User's Manual (*2008*)

WHAT OBJECTS MEAN
An Introduction to Material Culture (*2009*)

TOURISM IN JAPAN
An Ethno-Semiotic Analysis (*2010*)

THE CULTURAL THEORIST'S BOOK OF QUOTATIONS (*2010*)

THE OBJECTS OF AFFECTION
Semiotics and Consumer Culture (*2010*)

UNDERSTANDING AMERICAN ICONS
An Introduction to Semiotics (*2012*)

MEDIA, MYTH AND SOCIETY (*2012*)

THEORIZING TOURISM (*2012*)

BALI TOURISM (*2013*)

A YEAR AMONGST THE UK (*2013*)

DICTIONARY OF ADVERTISING AND MARKETING CONCEPTS (*2013*)

MESSAGES: AN INTRODUCTION TO COMMUNICATION (*2014*)

DOI: 10.1057/9781137565457.0001

palgrave▸pivot

Gizmos or: The Electronic Imperative: How Digital Devices have Transformed American Character and Culture

Arthur Asa Berger

Professor Emeritus of Broadcast and Electronic Communication Arts, San Francisco State University, USA

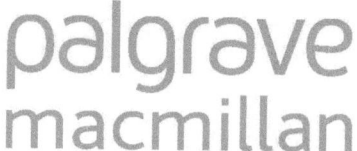

DOI: 10.1057/9781137565457.0001

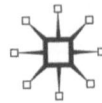

GIZMOS OR: THE ELECTRONIC IMPERATIVE
Copyright © Arthur Asa Berger, 2015.

All rights reserved.

First published in 2015 by

PALGRAVE MACMILLAN®
in the United States—a division of St. Martin's Press LLC,
175 Fifth Avenue, New York, NY 10010.

Where this book is distributed in the UK, Europe and the rest of the world,
this is by Palgrave Macmillan, a division of Macmillan Publishers Limited,
registered in England, company number 785998, of Houndmills, Basingstoke,
Hampshire RG21 6XS.

Palgrave Macmillan is the global academic imprint of the above companies
and has companies and representatives throughout the world.

Palgrave® and Macmillan® are registered trademarks in the United States,
the United Kingdom, Europe and other countries.

ISBN: 978–1–137–56546–4 EPUB
ISBN: 978–1–137–56545–7 PDF
ISBN: 978–1–137–57526–5 Hardback

Library of Congress Cataloging-in-Publication Data is available from the
Library of Congress.

A catalogue record of the book is available from the British Library.

First edition: 2015

www.palgrave.com/pivot

DOI: 10.1057/9781137565457

In memory of William Fry, Jr.

DOI: 10.1057/9781137565457.0001

Things are in the saddle,
And ride mankind.
There are two laws discrete
Not reconciled,
Law for man and law for thing:
The last builds town and fleet,
But it runs wild,
And doth the man unking.

Ralph Waldo Emerson
From "Ode to William Channing"

DOI: 10.1057/9781137565457.0001

Contents

List of Figures   viii

List of Tables   ix

Preface: Alone with My Thoughts   x

Acknowledgments   xiii

About the Author   xiv

Introduction: Why I Decided to Write This Book   1

1   The Internet: *Everyone Is Connected*   10

2   Smartphones: *Everyone Can Do Anything*   25

3   Television: *Everyone's Watching*   36

4   Tablet Computers: *Everyone's a God*   49

5   Computers: *Everyone's a Writer*   58

6   Video Game Consoles and Video Games: *Everyone's a Hero*   65

7   Digital Watches and Smart Watches: *Everyone's Monitored*   75

8   Digital Cameras and Photography: *Everyone's a Documentary Maker*   84

9   Computer Printers: *Everyone's a Publisher*   91

10   Flatbed Computer Scanners: *Everyone's an Art Director*   96

Coda   106

References   108

Index   110

DOI: 10.1057/9781137565457.0001

List of Figures

I.1   Some of my digital devices   3

I.2   The iceberg representation of the
human psyche   4

I.3   Jean Baudrillard   5

I.4   Electronic recharge icon   7

2.1   Smartphone   27

2.2   Erik Erikson   30

3.1   Football stadium   42

3.2   Baseball player   44

4.1   Medusa   53

4.2   Theseus and the Minotaur   54

5.1   Scene from Macintosh "1984" television
commercial   60

5.2   My Dell computer and Canon scanner   61

10.1   Scan from *signs in contemporary culture*   101

10.2   Karl Marx   102

10.3   Roland Barthes   102

10.4   Cover of book on English character
and culture   103

10.5   Still life 1: scanner pastiche by the author   104

DOI: 10.1057/9781137565457.0002

List of Tables

P.1   Use of media by adults   xi

2.1   Psychological crises and smartphone   31

3.1   Kinds of television sets and their prices   37

3.2   Statistics on television viewing   45

5.1   Worldwide sales of computers, tablets, and mobile phones   63

6.1   Kinds of video games   69

6.2   Worldwide sales of video games   69

6.3   Top ten video games in the United States   70

DOI: 10.1057/9781137565457.0003

Preface: Alone with My Thoughts

This book is an interpretation (some might say a highly idiosyncratic and in some cases a far-fetched interpretation) of the digital devices that play such an important role in our everyday lives. It uses semiotic, psychoanalytic, sociological, and Marxist ideological theories to analyze and better understand the function and impact of these digital devices on American society and culture. It is written in an accessible, conversational style, and is somewhat like a documentary in that it uses many quotations from writers and scholars who have interesting things to say that are relevant to my interests. I tend to follow theories where they lead me, so you might find, for example, my analysis of tablets, which ties them to myth and the Bible, fanciful. I have taken minor liberties with the punctuation of the quotations I use and have run paragraphs together to save space, but I have not changed them in any other manner.

There is no way to keep up with the changes in models of our electronic gizmos and in the software programs that run them. It seems like every day I get an email informing me that a new version of some software program I'm using is available. At the same time, I receive messages about new models of smartphones, printers, computers, and other devices that succeed one another with incredible rapidity.

And the newspapers are full of articles about these gizmos: how many iPhones Apple has sold, new smartphones from

DOI: 10.1057/9781137565457.0004

Google, new this, and new that. What has been the impact of these continuing changes in our software programs and in the gizmos that use them? And what do these endlessly updated software programs and models of our gizmos reflect about American culture and society?

Recently some research was done in which people were asked to sit in a room and be alone with their thoughts. If this was unpleasant for them, they could give themselves "painful" electronic shocks. What the researchers discovered was that around 60% of the males and 30% of the females being tested preferred to administer shocks to themselves than sit alone with their thoughts. An article by Gregory Barber, "Surrounded By Digital Distractions, We Can't Even Stop to Think" (July 3, 2014, "AllTech Considered," NPR) describes the experiment:

> In a study to appear in Thursday's issue [July 10, 2014] of the journal *Science*, participants found the experience within their own heads surprisingly difficult to manage—if not downright unpleasant. Stripped of their books, cellphones and other distractions, many, including a majority of men, preferred to instead pass the time by reaching for the sole form of electronic entertainment in the room: a 9-volt battery administering a "severe static shock" when touched.

And that's where we are now. People are so dependent upon their digital gizmos that rather than sit in a room, without them, and think, they prefer to give themselves "painful" shocks.

The figures on our use of electronic media are remarkable. Nielsen offers the following statistics (my construction) on the use of electronic media by adults (eighteen and older):

TABLE P.1   *Use of media by adults*

05.04 hours	Live television
02.46 hours	Radio
01:07 hours	Smartphones
01:01 hours	Internet on a PC
00:32 hours	Time-shifted television
00:12 hours	Game consoles

I left out a couple of minor items from the list. This adds up to around eleven hours a day that we spend with electronic media, though because many people multitask, it ends up an hour or so less for them.

DOI: 10.1057/9781137565457.0004

A friend of mine recently told me "I love my iPhone." Why do we "love" our iPhones or other brands of smartphones? Is there, I ask, some kind of an electronic imperative in which our devices foster certain kinds of relationships with us that may not be healthy or positive? We know what our digital gizmos can do for us. But what are they doing to us?

DOI: 10.1057/9781137565457.0004

Acknowledgments

I would like to thank my editor, Shaun Vigil, my editorial assistant, Erica Buchman, and the editorial and production staff of Palgrave Macmillan for their assistance in publishing this book. I would also like to thank the reviewer of this book for supporting and offering many valuable suggestions. I owe an enormous debt to all the technology writers and other writers whose insights have guided me in writing this book and whose work I have cited. I have a number of quotations from these writers that reflect their style of writing and their ideas. Finally, I have to express my admiration for all the scientists, engineers, software writers, and designers who have created the digital devices I discuss in this book.

About the Author

Arthur Asa Berger is Professor Emeritus of Broadcast and Electronic Communication Arts at San Francisco State University, where he taught from 1965 until 2003. He has a BA in Literature from the University of Massachusetts, an MA in Journalism from the University of Iowa (where he also studied at the Writers Workshop), and a PhD from the University of Minnesota, in American Studies in 1965. He wrote his dissertation on the comic strip *Li'l Abner*. During the 1963–1964 academic year, he had a Fulbright grant to Italy and taught at the University of Milan. He spent a year as a visiting professor at the Annenberg School for Communication at the University of Southern California in Los Angeles in 1984 and taught a short- course on advertising in 2002 as a Fulbright Senior Specialist at the Heinrich Heine University in Düsseldorf, Germany. In 2012 he spent a month lecturing in Argentina on semiotics and media criticism as a Fulbright Senior Specialist. In 2014 he spent a month as a Fulbright Senior Specialist at Belarus State University lecturing on discourse analysis, media criticism, and popular culture.

He is the author of more than 140 articles and book reviews, and of more than seventy books on the mass media, popular culture, humor, and everyday life. Among his recent books are *Media Analysis Techniques,* 5th edition; *Seeing I is Believing: An Introduction to Visual Communication,* 4th edition; *Understanding American Icons: An Introduction to Semiotics; The Art of Comedy Writing; Messages: An Introduction to Communication* and *Media, Myth and Society.* He has also written a number of academic mysteries: *The*

DOI: 10.1057/9781137565457.0006

Hamlet Case, *Postmortem for a Postmodernist*, *The Mass Comm Murders: Five Media Theorists Self-Destruct*, and *Durkheim Is Dead: Sherlock Holmes Is Introduced to Social Theory*. His books have been translated into German, Swedish, Italian, Korean, Indonesian, Farsi, Arabic, Turkish, and Chinese. He has lectured in more than a dozen countries in the course of his career. Berger is married, has two children and four grandchildren, and lives in Mill Valley, California.

DOI: 10.1057/9781137565457.0006

palgrave▸**pivot**

www.palgrave.com/pivot

Introduction: Why I Decided to Write This Book

Abstract: *I became aware of the role digital devices play in our lives in an airport in Cancun, Mexico while watching two men discuss and display their various devices. It occurred to me that there is some kind of a force, which I call "the electronic imperative," that may be operating in our unconscious that derives important gratifications from having and using digital devices or one kind or another. I reference work by a professor at the Harvard Business School about what he calls the "95-5 Split" in our minds, with the ninety-five figure being our unconscious, which, he argues, shapes much of our behavior. I used the term "gizmos" because it is a common term that we use for devices whose name we momentarily forget and quote the French sociologist Jean Baudrillard who explains that gizmos are getting more complicated and tend to dominate us. I then quote from Ernest Dichter, the father of motivation research, who explains that objects tell us a great deal about ourselves. Finally, I discuss the meaning of digital by quoting from Peter Lunenfeld's book,* The Digital Dialectic, *on the meaning of "digital."*

Berger, Arthur Asa. *Gizmos or: The Electronic Imperative: How Digital Devices have Transformed American Character and Culture.* New York: Palgrave Macmillan, 2015.
DOI: 10.1057/9781137565457.0007.

A Nielsen report on the importance of digital devices in our lives sets the stage for my investigation of the role they play in our lives.

> Technology has changed a lot in the last 30 years—even the last three! Today's consumer is more connected than ever, thanks to the proliferation of digital devices and platforms. Content once available only via specific channels, such as print and broadcast television, can today be delivered to consumers through their multiple connected devices. These changes are driving a media revolution and blurring traditional media definitions. In fact, Americans now own four digital devices on average, and the average U.S. consumer spends 60 hours a week consuming content across devices. In Nielsen's Digital Consumer Report, we explore this transformation and examine how the everyday lives of consumers are now intertwined with the digital world. At the heart of this shift is the proliferation of digital devices. A majority of U.S. households now own High-Definition Televisions (HDTVs), Internet-connected computers and smartphones, giving consumer more choices for how and when they access content. Two-thirds of Americans now use smartphones, allowing them to take media content wherever they want, and they also to use the devices throughout their purchase journey.
>
> http://www.nielsen.com/us/en/newswire/2014/whats-empowering-the-new-digital-consumer.html

On January 22, 2014, I was sitting in the airport at Puerto Vallarta with my wife, waiting to catch a plane to San Francisco when a man of around sixty, who we shall call John Doe, sat down on a seat facing me. His wife, Jane Doe, sat down next to him. Then a man of about seventy, sat down next to John Doe's wife. John Doe had a Kindle in his hand and was looking at it. The man who had just sat down then asked John Doe about the E-Reader. "I love it," John Doe said. "It lights up at night so you can read in a dark room...and one charge lasts for months." Then John Doe took an Apple mini iPad from a small bag. "The resolution on this thing is fantastic," he added. Then he pulled out a light metal (aluminum) laptop and showed it to the man. "This one isn't an Apple. But it weighs almost nothing." The other man then pulled out an Apple laptop to show him. "This is what I use. I really love it," he said, and they continued discussing their electronic gismos until everyone boarded the plane.

When I watched the two men talking about their electronic devices, I became aware of the extent to which digital electronic gizmos of one kind or another have impacted on the lives of not only our younger generations but also people of more advanced ages. We are, it would seem, all plugged in—with many different digital devices that play an

DOI: 10.1057/9781137565457.0007

increasingly important role in our lives. I am over eighty and I have a Dell desktop computer, an HP laptop computer, a fifteen-inch Toshiba laptop, two Brother printers, a ten-inch ASUS tablet, a Nexus 4 smartphone, two Canon digital cameras, a Canon digital scanner, two digital watches, and four MP3 players. My wife has a ten-inch ASUS tablet and also a Nexus 7 digital tablet and a Motorola smartphone. In addition, we have three microwave ovens (one that we use all the time and two others we picked up over the years for one reason or another), a digital dishwasher, a digital washing machine, a digital clothes dryer, a digital bread maker, and who knows how many other digital gizmos in the house. The important message to take from this description of some of the objects in my house is that I am typical of many middle-class or upper-middle-class Americans and many Americans have many more electronic gizmos than my wife and I have (Figure I.1).

There is, I would suggest, an electronic imperative that plays an increasingly larger role in our everyday lives. In this book, my focus will be on what these digital gizmos reveal about our culture, about the role they play in our lives and our society, and about their hidden meanings. Sociologists make a distinction between manifest and latent functions. Manifest functions are obvious and latent functions are hidden and ones that we are unaware of. In the same light, psychoanalytic culture theorists distinguish between consciousness—those elements of our psyche of which we are aware—and the unconscious—those elements of our

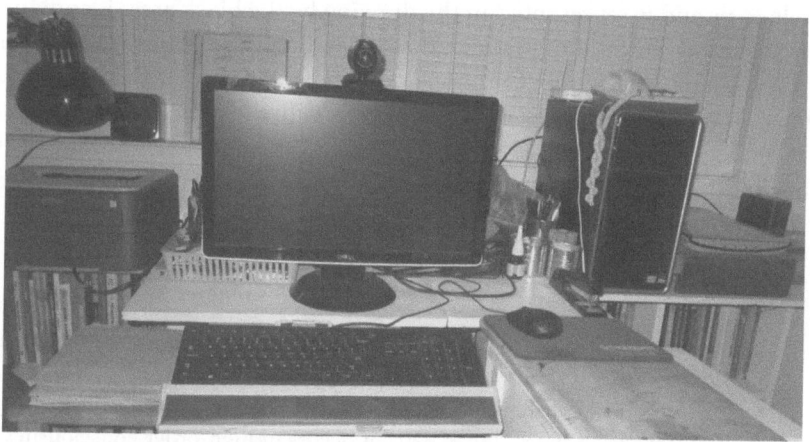

FIGURE I.1   *Some of my digital devices*

DOI: 10.1057/9781137565457.0007

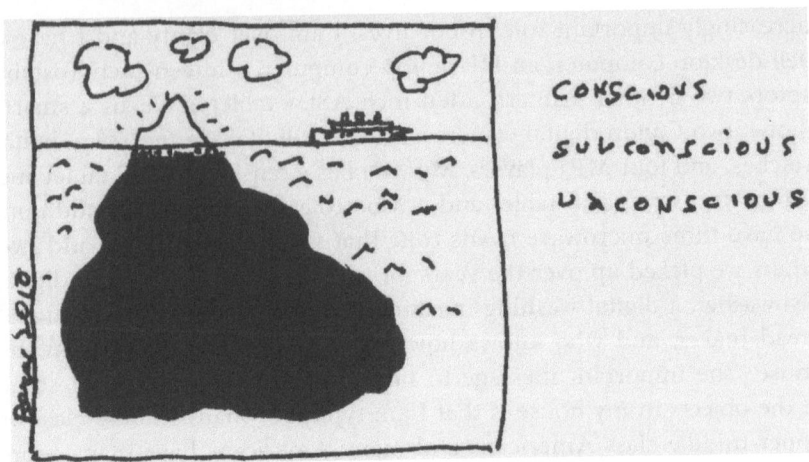

FIGURE I.2   *The iceberg representation of the human psyche*

psyche of which we are unaware, but, if Freud is right, play an important role in shaping our behavior (Figure I.2).

Let's take an iceberg as representing the human psyche. Consciousness is what we are aware of, the part of the iceberg we can see; the subconscious contains material that is just below the level of our consciousness that we can access. In the iceberg representing our psyches, it would be up to five or six feet below the level of the sea, and is the part of the iceberg that we can dimly make out. But the unconscious is not accessible to us and is represented in the drawing by the black area. It contains an enormous amount of material that we are unaware of but which plays an important role in our thinking and behavior. Many of the things we do are motivated by unconscious imperatives in our psyches.

Gerald Zaltman, a professor at the Harvard Business School, suggests that most of our behavior is shaped by unconscious processes. In his book, *How Customers Think: Essential Insights into the Mind of the Market* (2003: 50) he writes:

The 95-5 Split

Consciousness is crucial in daily life for many obvious reasons. However, an important fact and one of the key principles of this book is the 95-5 split. At least 95 percent of all cognition appears below awareness in the shadows of the mind while, at most, only 5 percent occurs in high-order consciousness. Many disciplines have confirmed this insight.

DOI: 10.1057/9781137565457.0007

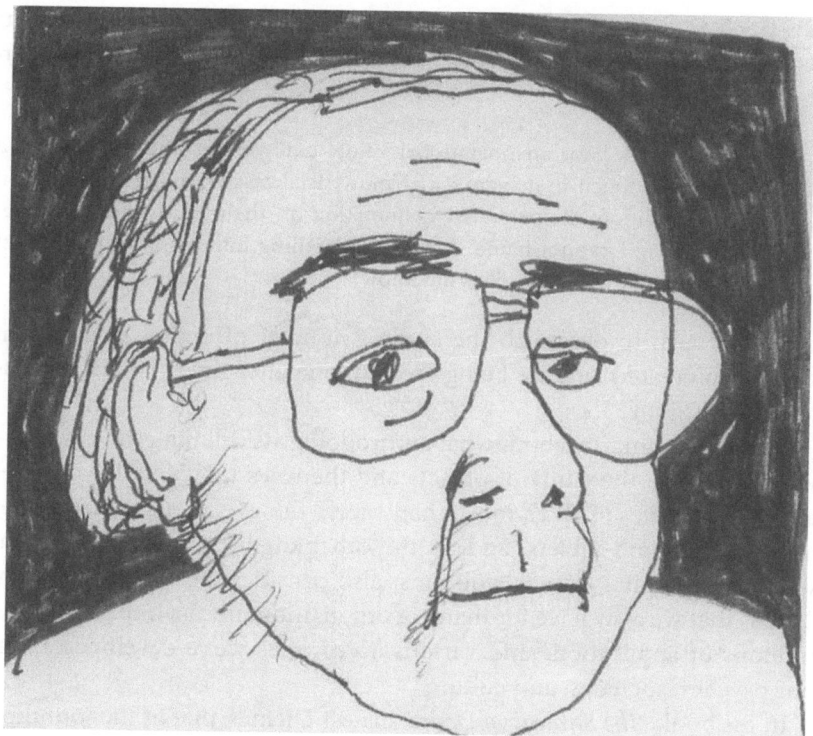

FIGURE I.3   *Jean Baudrillard*

This material in our unconscious, in "the shadows of the mind," has a profound impact on our decision-making and behavior in general and, in particular, when it comes to purchasing digital devices (Figure I.3).

Jean Baudrillard, the French sociologist-semiotician, makes an interesting point about the objects and gizmos we use in his books *The System of Objects*: they have become increasingly complex and powerful and many of them seem to have turned us into their slaves. He writes (1996: 56):

> A genuine revolution has taken place on the everyday plane: *objects have now become more complex than human behaviour relative to them.* Objects are more and more highly differentiated—our gestures less and less so. To put it another way: objects are no longer surrounded by the theatre of gesture in which they used to be simply the various roles; instead their emphatic goal-directedness has very nearly turned them into the actors in a global process in which *man* is merely the role, or the spectator.

DOI: 10.1057/9781137565457.0007

His book is a classic study of the role of objects and developments in technology in our everyday lives. He explains what gizmos are later in the book (1996: 114):

> A gizmo does have an operational value, but whereas the function of a machine is explicit in its name, a gizmo....is always an indeterminate term with, in addition, the pejorative connotation of "the thing without a name" or "the thing I cannot name" (there is something immoral about an object whose exact purpose one does not know).

I use the term to deal with the endless number of digital devices that have been created and are being created, one after the other, in endless profusion (Figure I.4).

Gizmos is primarily about what anthropologists call material culture— which involves the study of objects and the roles they play in our lives and our societies. There's more than meets the eye about smartphones and phablets and tablets, and all the other digital gizmos. When you write about digital gizmos, you must also consider the various software "Apps" that we now have for many of our gizmos and the impact of these millions of applications and various accessories we've developed upon our psyches, societies, and culture.

In his book, *The Strategy of Desire*, Ernest Dichter, one of the founding fathers of motivation research, discusses the power of objects and their psychological meaning for us. He writes (2002: 91):

> The knowledge of the soul of things is possibly a very direct and new and revolutionary way of discovering the soul of man. The power of various types of objects to bring out into the open new aspects of the personality of modern man is great. The more intimate knowledge of as many different types of products a man has, the richer his life will be.... In the final analysis objects motivate our life probably at least as much as the Oedipus complex or childhood experiences do.

For Dichter, objects play a much more important role in our lives than we may imagine and they enable students of objects, marketing consultants, and advertising executives, to gain insights into our motives and desires of which we are often unaware.

The term "gizmo" is conventionally used for gadgets whose name we cannot recall, so we evade the problem of remembering which electronic device we are thinking about and use the term "gizmo." Thus, for example,

DOI: 10.1057/9781137565457.0007

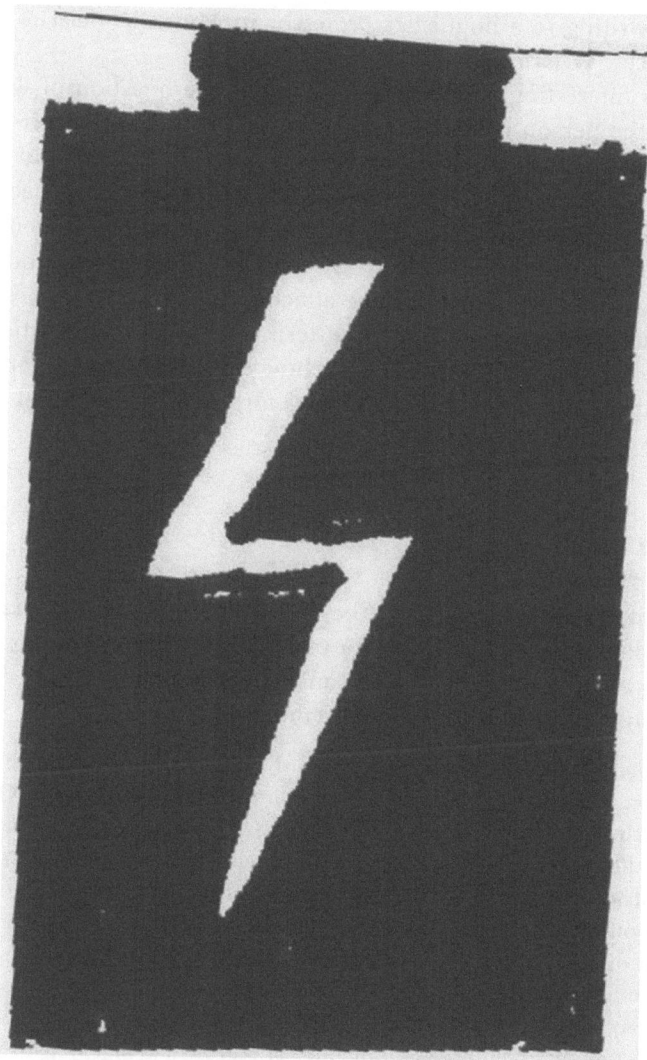

FIGURE I.4 *Electronic recharge icon*

someone might be talking about an MP3 player but can't remember the name of the object or its brand and say "I have this gizmo that I use to listen to music." I use gizmo because it covers a whole range of digital electronic devices and people in the United States generally understand what you are talking about when you use the term. I happen to use the

DOI: 10.1057/9781137565457.0007

term in writing to a linguistics professor in Minsk in Belarus and she wrote back, "What's a gizmo?"

What's interesting about digital gizmos is the question of who is in control: the person using the gizmo or the gizmo? A number of years ago I went to a lecture on computers by a social scientist and he used the term "servoproteins" to describe the relation between people and computers. His argument is that we human beings (the proteins) have become the servants of our electronic gizmos in many ways, and anyone who has seen how people become attached to their gizmos—especially their smartphones—might find the term fitting. I've read articles that describe the way many teenage girls now sleep with their smartphones next to them, and turned on—lest, God forbid, they miss a call or a text message.

A note on the digital

The term "digital" comes from the term we use for the fingers on our hands—known as digits. A scholar of all things digital, Peter Lunenfeld, explains what the term digital means in his book *The Digital Dialectic: New Essays on New Media.* He writes (1999: xv):

> Digital systems do not use continuously variable representational relation-ships. Instead, they translate all input into binary structures of Os and Is, which can then be stored, transferred, or manipulated at the level or numbers of "digits" (so called because etymologically, the word descends form the digits on our hand with which we count out those numbers). Thus a phone call on a digital system will be encoded as a series of these Os and Is and sent over the wires as binary information to be reinterpreted as speech on the other end.... It is the capacity of the electronic computer to encode a vast variety of information digitally that has given it such a central place within contemporary culture. As all manner of representational systems are recast as digital information, then all can be stored, accessed, and controlled by the same equipment. (Cambridge, MA: MIT Press)

The argument of my book is that the digital revolution has had a major impact of every aspect of life in contemporary society, from smart-phones to television sets to tablets, video game consoles, and social media. We now live in a digital age, which has led to remarkable trans-formations and new developments in many areas of our lives, societies, and culture.

DOI: 10.1057/9781137565457.0007

We become attached to these devices and, in a recent movie, *Her*, one of the characters falls in love with one of them—or, more precisely, the voice of the computer operating system (Scarlet Johannsen) coming from his computer. Some of my friends who have told me, many times, how much they love their iPhones, might not find the premise of this film that ridiculous.

DOI: 10.1057/9781137565457.0007

1

The Internet: *Everyone Is Connected*

Abstract: *This chapter offers a definition of the Internet (of which there are many), a timeline on the development the Internet and devices that make use of it, and of various sociocultural issues connected with the Internet, such as the problem of privacy in the Internet age, the social problem of bullying by people using the Internet, and the impact the Internet has had on our psyches—especially in relation to loneliness and isolation that afflict many people. It also deals with addiction to video games and the forthcoming "Internet of Things," in which all of our digital devices will be connected to one another and can be operated with our smartphones.*

Berger, Arthur Asa. *Gizmos or: The Electronic Imperative: How Digital Devices have Transformed American Character and Culture.* New York: Palgrave Macmillan, 2015.
DOI: 10.1057/9781137565457.0008.

DOI: 10.1057/9781137565457.0008

I begin with two quotations that offer different perspectives on the role that the Internet plays in our lives and the impact the Internet has had on our societies and cultures. You can decide, as you read this book, which interpretation makes most sense to you. The first quotation is by Howard Rheingold, and is taken from his book *Net Smart: How to Thrive Online.*

> Mass collaboration has transformed not only the way people use the Internet but also how information is found (Google's PageRank), knowledge is aggregated (Wikipedia), science is conducted (citizen science), software is created (social production of the free Linux operating system and Firefox, the second most popular Web browser), computing power is harnessed for research (distributed computation), people are entertained (massive multiplayer online games), problems are solved (collective intelligence), news is gathered (citizen journalism), disaster relief is delivered (crisis mapping and emergent collective response), communities are formed (virtual communities), and commercial products are designed and tested (crowdsourcing). It isn't easy to think of a realm of human behavior that has not been influenced in some way by some form of mass collaboration.
>
> Howard Rheingold, *Net Smart: How to Thrive Online.*

The second is by a philosopher, Herbert Dreyfus, and comes from his book *On the Internet.* He is much more critical than Rheingold is about the impact of the Internet on our lives, our relationships with our families and related concerns.

> The research examined the social and psychological impact of the Internet on 169 people in seventy-three households during their first one or two years online....In this sample, the Internet was used extensively for communication. Nonetheless, the greater use of the Internet was associated with declines in participants' communication with family members in the household, declines in the size of their social circle, and increases in depression and loneliness....On-line friendships are likely to be more limited than friendships supported by physical proximity....Because on-line friends are not embedded in the same day-to-day environment, they will be less likely to understand the context for conversation, making discussion more difficult and rendering support less applicable.
>
> Even strong ties maintained at a distance through electronic communication are likely to be different in kind and perhaps diminished in strength compared with strong ties supported by physical proximity. The interpersonal communication applications currently prevalent on the Internet are either neutral toward strong ties or tend to undercut them rather than promote them.

DOI: 10.1057/9781137565457.0008

I was thirty-six years old when the Internet first began, in a primitive way, as a result of an initiative by the United States Government's ARPA—Advanced Research Projects Agency—and I was sixty-five when Google was created. Unlike my children and grandchildren, I did not grow up with the Internet and all the digital gizmos—the subject of this book—that make use of it and digital technology. I bought my first computer, a Commodore 64, in 1982 (if I recall correctly) for $600, which means I can be classified as an "early adopter" of computers. It enabled me to do very primitive word processing, but once I learned how to use the computer for word processing I began buying more powerful computers—ones that could use other programs such as Word Perfect and then various iterations of Microsoft Word.

My Gizmos

This book is being typed on a Dell Inspiron computer with Windows 8.1. I am using Word 2013. I have, in addition to the gizmos I listed earlier, a WD external hard disk, and a Sharp Fax machine. As I explained earlier, I have many gizmos: I have an AT&T modem/router for our Wi-Fi. I've had a succession of cheap cell phones over the past ten or fifteen years and finally was tempted by the incredible capacities of smartphones and purchased a smartphone, a Google Nexus 4. Having written about smartphones, I decided, finally, to get one. It is an amazing device, with apps that can count how many steps I've taken and others that I can use to photograph checks so I can deposit them directly, over the Internet. Recently our daughter gave us three Vtech telephones so now we have four regular telephones and three Vtech telephones in the house. In many rooms we now have two telephones: a traditional landline and a Vtech portable telephone.

For a number of years I used Netgear's technical computer support, which was done by phone using 800 numbers to call India. Netgear has a program, Bomgar, which enables technicians in India to take control of a computer and make repairs. But I switched to Microsoft technical support, in part because they have a Microsoft store near where I live, which means I don't have to wait to be connected to a Netgear technician in India. The technicians were excellent but in recent months it took almost an hour to get connected to one. I got tired of the long waits on the phone (originally you'd be connected very quickly) so I decided to use Microsoft's computer repair service.

DOI: 10.1057/9781137565457.0008

It is the Internet (some spell it with a small "i" as the internet) that is central to the creation of many, if not most, of the fantastic digital electronic devices that play such a large role in our lives nowadays. I've always felt there is some kind of an imperative connected with the digital gizmos we use. Is there some kind of a connection between the electricity in our brains and our digital gizmos that helps explain why we become so involved with them? In this chapter, I will deal with the Internet and its impact on our psyches, societies, and cultures. The Pew Research Trust reports that in 2000, 52% of adults used the Internet. For 2015, the figure is 84%, a considerable increase. For more details, see Pew Research, July 02, 2015.

The electronic imperative

I have suggested earlier that there is an electronic imperative that plays a role that we may not be aware of in our daily lives. I believe that the creation of the Internet marks a turning point in human history, so we can say life that existed before the Internet had a certain quality but our lives after the Internet are radically different from what they were before the Internet.

Virginia Woolf described a similarly important change in 1924, at a lecture she gave at the Heretics Club at Cambridge University in 1924. She said:

> On or about December, 1910, human character changed. I am not saying that one went out, as one might into a garden, and there saw a rose had flowered, or that a hen had laid an egg. The change was not like that. But a change there was, nevertheless, and since one must be arbitrary, let us date it about the year 1910... When human relations change, there is at the same time a change in religion, conduct, politics, and literature.

Woolf argued that after December 1910 (or around then) life in England had changed in major ways—a change that she noticed in the relationships between husbands and wives, masters and servants, children and parents, and the kind of literature that was being written. Scholars have described this change as the advent of modernism.

We can make a similar statement about the invention of the Internet and suggest that "On or about December 1983, when the Internet was invented, human society and culture changed." There is some question

DOI: 10.1057/9781137565457.0008

about when the Internet actually came into being but I will take 1983 as the date. A year or two, one way or another, doesn't really matter. What is important is that after the Internet was invented, life changed in remarkable ways. I will deal with the smartphone, the most revolutionary and important device that uses the Internet, shortly. After I try to define the Internet.

Let me begin with a quotation that answers the question "What is the Internet?" After that, I will offer timeline that lists some of the major points in the creation and evolution of the Internet. Then I will discuss its impact.

What is the Internet?

I got this description of the Internet from a site on the Internet, http://www.merriam-webster.com/dictionary/internet. Here is the description they offered:

> Publicly accessible computer NETWORK connecting many smaller networks from around the world. It grew out of a U.S. Defense Department program called ARPANET (Advanced Research Projects Agency Network), established in 1969 with connections between computers at the University of California at Los Angeles, Stanford Research Institute, the University of California-Santa Barbara, and the University of Utah. ARPANET's purpose was to conduct research into computer networking in order to provide a secure and survivable communications system in case of war. As the network quickly expanded, academics and researchers in other fields began to use it as well. In 1971 the first program for sending E-MAIL over a distributed network was developed; by 1973, the year international connections to ARPANET were made (from Britain and Norway), e-mail represented most of the traffic on ARPANET. The 1970s also saw the development of mailing lists, NEWSGROUPS and BULLETIN-BOARD SYSTEMS, and the TCP/IP communications PROTO-COLS, which were adopted as standard protocols for ARPANET in 1982–1983, leading to the widespread use of the term Internet. In 1984 the DOMAIN NAME addressing system was introduced. In 1986 the National Science Foundation established the NSFNET, a distributed network of networks capable of handling far greater traffic, and within a year more than 10,000 hosts were connected to the Internet. In 1988 real-time conversation over the network became possible with the development of Internet Relay Chat protocols (*see* CHAT). In 1990 ARPANET ceased to exist, leaving behind the NSFNET, and the first commercial dial-up access to the Internet became available. In 1991, the World was released to the public (via FTP). The Mosaic BROWSER was

DOI: 10.1057/9781137565457.0008

released in 1993, and its popularity led to the proliferation of World Wide Web sites and users.

This description/definition also offers some interesting historical information about the development of the Internet. In essence, the Internet is a vast network that links smaller computer networks that can transmit words, sounds, and images in a bewildering number of programs.

Timeline on the Internet

This timeline is based on a number of different timelines available on the Internet, some of which are very long and detailed and others of which are short and lack detail. I've put some of them together in the timeline that follows.

1822   Computer prototype developed by Charles Babbage
1939   First modern computer designed by John Vincent Atanasoff at Iowa State University
1951   UNIVAC, first civilian computer created by Eckert and Mauchly
1969   ARPA (Advanced Research Projects Agency) connects four major US universities in December
1972   Pong, the first video game, created
1972   Electronic mail introduced by Ray Tomlinson who uses the @ to distinguish between the sender's name and network name in the email address
1973   Transmission Control Protocol/Internet Protocol (TCP/IP)
1978   Cellular phone service starts
1982   The word "Internet" is first used
1984   Domain Name System (DNS) created. Network addresses identified by extensions such as .com, .org, and .edu
1984   Writer William Gibson coins the Term "cyberspace".
1984   Apple Macintosh computer introduced
1983   TCP/IP becomes standard. FTP (File Transfer Protocol) developed so users can download files from a different computer
1985   America Online, debuts, offers email, electronic bulletin boards, news, and other information
1988   Internet Worm virus shuts down about 10% of the world's Internet servers

DOI: 10.1057/9781137565457.0008

1989	Tim Berners-Lee of CERN (European Laboratory for Particle Physics) develops the World Wide Web, based on hypertext, for distributing information on the Internet. The Web can now be accessed by a graphical user interface
1991	Gopher interface is created at the University of Minnesota
1993	HTML develops, Internet opens to commercial use
1993	Marc Andreessen develops Mosaic at the National Center for Supercomputing Applications (NCSA)
1994	The White House launches its website, www.whitehouse.gov
1994	Internet vocabulary adds the term "spamming"
1994	Navigator browser and Netscape Communication created by Marc Andreessen and Jim Clark
1994	Amazon.com launched by Jeff Bezos
1995	CompuServe, America Online, and Prodigy started
1995	Sun Microsystems releases the Internet programming language called Java
1995	First digital phones
1997	The term "weblog" is coined, becomes "blog"
1997	Netflix created
1998	Google opens its first office, in California
1999	MySpace.com is launched
2000	Viruses now become a problem
2001	Birth of Wikipedia
2003	Spam becomes a big problem
2003	Apple Computer creates Apple iTunes Music Store
2004	Facebook is created
2005	YouTube.com is launched
2006	There are more than 92 million websites online
2007	Online game, World of Warcraft, has more than 9 million subscribers worldwide
2007	Apple iPhone introduced
2010	Apple iPad introduced
2011	Sixteen billion indexed Web pages on Internet
2012	Google Glass, wearable computers become popular
2012	Advanced Smart Watches
2014	Occulus Virtual Reality Headphone
2014	"Right to be forgotten" ruling in Europe
2015	Apple Smart Watch

DOI: 10.1057/9781137565457.0008

As I write this, Facebook now has almost 1.2 billion members and it recently purchased WhatsApp, a popular messaging company with around sixty employees (now all millionaires and billionaires), for 19 billion dollars. Currently around 450 million people use WhatsApp (including myself) and on December 31, 2013 WhatsApp handled 44 billion messages.

Things in the technology world move very quickly. New versions of smart watches are being developed one after another (many of which are designed to monitor our bodies) and other wearable computers are becoming popular. Some theorists suggest that wearable computers will be the most important development in the future and we'll ditch our desktops, laptops, tablets, and smartphones for smart watches and other wearable devices. Our bodies develop and change relatively slowly, once we reach adolescence, but our technologies develop rapidly, with a new models of gizmos often appearing shortly after an earlier model appeared and there is no end in sight in terms of the way gizmos and software apps keep changing.

The loyalty to teenagers also tends to be rather fickle. As I understand things, from talking with some teenagers, they are bored with Facebook and texting and now are fascinated with instant messaging and Instagram. They are always waiting for the new "hot" app and change their loyalties quickly. So just because some teenagers are abandoning Facebook doesn't mean it is doomed to eventually fade away.

Issues with the Internet

The quotes that begins this chapter, by Howard Rheingold, a futurist, and Hubert L. Dreyfus, a philosophy professor, offer insights into the reach of the Internet and its impact upon many aspects of our lives. Rheingold is positive about the potentials of the Internet and Dreyfus is guarded, citing a research project that found that families that used the Internet spent less time with one another and members of these families often felt lonely. At a recent social event my wife and I attended, I noticed a number of people were using their smartphones. A little girl of seven or eight was using her mother's smartphone, a boy of about twelve was occupied with a tablet, and several college students were looking at their phones. I asked one young woman, a college student, who had just taken her smartphone out of her purse how much she used her phone. "Not

DOI: 10.1057/9781137565457.0008

that much," she said. It then turned out she is on it for around three hours a day and sends her friends a hundred text messages a day.

There are any number of issues that the Internet raises. For one thing, there is the question of privacy and of the intrusive nature of governmental agencies, such as the National Security Agency (NSA) in the United States and other spy agencies in other countries. As a result of the files downloaded by Edward J. Snowden, we now know that the NSA has been collecting emails and phone calls by Americans and others to a degree we hadn't realized. On February 28, 2014 *The New York Times* carried a story, based on information leaked by Snowden, that shows the extent to which spy agencies are invading our privacy. The story, written by Nicole Perlroth and Vindu Goel (page B1) discussed invasions of our privacy by a British spy agency:

> A British intelligence agency collected video webcam images—many of them sexually explicit—from millions of Yahoo users, regardless of whether they were suspected of illegal activity, according to accounts of documents leaked by Edward J. Snowden.

The article, titled "British Spies Said to Intercept Yahoo Webcam Images," adds that it is not known whether the agency shared this information with the NSA or intercepted material from Google Hangouts or Microsoft Skype. The article said that the British spy agency was investigating how to use cameras in Microsoft Kinect devices, used with Microsoft Xbox game consoles, to spy on people playing games on their Xboxes.

The Problem of privacy

We can see the question of privacy being raised about our participation in Facebook and other similar sites, in which we may provide information about our private lives that shouldn't be made public. I know I continually receive email messages from organizations such as CNET that can teach us how to protect our privacy and not make certain information available to others, who may wish to steal from us or harm us in one way or another. There has been a curious form of emailing called "sexting" in which men or women send images of themselves without clothes to others. Research indicates that young women who send nude photos of themselves to others tend to have sexual relations earlier than women who don't. A member of the House of Representatives from New York had to leave his office because of sexting images he sent to someone. This kind of behavior can do damage to one's reputation and also be

DOI: 10.1057/9781137565457.0008

repugnant to people who receive the sexted email. And as we saw above, sending sexually explicit images on Yahoo to friends often ends up being seen by more people than we might imagine.

Because it is difficult to control what people write in their emails and the kind of sites they create, the Internet is full of racist, anti-Semitic, and other similarly ugly and anti-social sites on Facebook and other places that are repellant and sometime dangerous. You can find instructions on how to make bombs on the Internet. You can find pornography on the Internet. In fact, you can find almost anything on the Internet. It is estimated that there are something like 3 billion pages on the Internet, with millions of pages being added each day.

Bullying on the Internet

Some young people use the Internet to bully others—sometime this cyberbullying is so bad that in some cases the bullied victims commit suicide. This cyberbullying takes the form of insults, gossip, and other hostile and negative statements that the bullies make. All of this is available to everyone and young people who do not have strong defenses against this kind of behavior suffer terribly. It is estimated that there are around 4 million pages of cyberbullying on Google. An example follows:

> CNN—A 17-year-old North Carolina boy was charged with cyberbullying Friday after he posted a nude photo of a 15-year-old girl to an Instagram site, the Rowan County Sheriff's Office reported.
>
> The sheriff's office said the girl sent the photograph to her boyfriend, who shared it with the suspect. The suspect put the photo on an Instagram site he created called TheseHoes01, the sheriff's office said.
>
> When deputies were alerted to the existence of the photo, they traced it back to the 17-year-old, a press release stated. He was questioned at West Rowan High School, where he's a student. Deputies said he was "open and honest about his actions and accepts responsibility." He was suspended from school after being charged.

This case is instructive because it shows that once an image is sent to someone, you can never tell what will happen to it. This story shows how dangerous sexting can be; the boyfriend who shared the image with the friend made a terrible mistake—though we can argue that the girl who sent a nude picture of herself was very gullible. The young man who posted the nude photo on Instagram under the title "TheseHoes01" was,

DOI: 10.1057/9781137565457.0008

in effect, calling the girl a whore. As this story, and the story about the British spies capturing sexually explicit images of people from Yahoo shows that images are always dangerous.

The problem of loneliness and isolation

In his book, *On the Internet*, Hubert L. Dreyfus quoted research to the effect that people using computers to communicate with others often felt depressed and lonely. In a chapter titled "Disembodied Telepresence and the Remoteness of the Real," he writes (2008: 49):

> We can keep up with the latest events in the universe, shop, do research, communicate with our family, friends and colleagues, meet new people, play games, and control remote robots all without leaving our rooms. When we are engaged in such activities, our bodies seem irrelevant and our minds seem to be present wherever our interest takes us.
>
> Some enthusiasts rejoice that, thanks to progress in achieving such telepresence, we are on the way to sloughing off our situated bodies and becoming ubiquitous and, ultimately, immortal. Others worry that if we stay in our rooms and only relate to the world and other people through the Net we will become isolated and depressed.

Dreyfus then quotes from a Stanford study in which the director of the study "asserted that the Internet was creating a broad new wave of social isolation in the United States, raising the specter of an atomized world without human contact or emotion" (Dreyfus, 2008: 49). People may become members of virtual communities and join other groups but that is not the same thing as having face-to-face interactions with real people.

In some countries, such as Korea, many young people have become so attached to their computers and interactions with others, or game playing, that special camps have been created to help them overcome their addictions to computers, the Internet, and game playing. In Korea playing video games is now seen as a sport that attracts thousands of people when tournaments are held. The parents of these addicted children complain that the computers have stolen their children from them. The reason people become addicted to the Internet and the millions of things available on it is that they derive certain gratifications from being on the Internet and having the power to do all kinds of things. Normal children and young adults generally can limit their time at the computer but for some people, who have psychological problems or problems with impulse control, this is not possible.

DOI: 10.1057/9781137565457.0008

We see this matter of being obsessed with the Internet and computers, with smartphones and tablets, which are powerful microcomputers. As I pointed out earlier, some adolescents send a hundred or more text messages to their friends every day. This takes a good deal of time and subjects the people sending the text messages to a certain amount of stress—since they have to appear cool and have to be careful as they don't like the wrong singers or offer opinions that may cause problems. Sherry Turkle, a media scholar at the Massachusetts Institute of Technology, has written about the deleterious effects of all this texting. There is an alienating aspect to it—you don't hear the sound of a human voice, you don't have to respond to others, the way you do on the telephone.

When we become interested in exploring some topic on the Internet, time often disappears and we spend much more time than we imagined we would. The result is that we spend less time directly interacting with our parents, siblings, and friends. We become detached spectators of the world rather than becoming part of it and acting in it. Human beings are social animals and being social animals suggests that we see ourselves as part of society and act in society rather than being disembodied spectators, observing society through various portals on the Internet.

There are a number of psychological problems connected with Internet use, one of which is addiction, which leads to other problems. This matter is described as follows:

> The addict become reliant upon the internet and loses self-control to the internet. Discontinued usage of the internet results in withdrawal symptoms such as disturbances in mood and behavior. The addict can acquire techno-stress after habituating to the accelerated sense of time on the computer. Its symptoms are "internalizing the standards by which the computer works: accelerated time, a desire for perfection, yes-no patterns of thinking." Studies reveal a strong link between excessive Internet use and serious mental disorders. For a study in the March 2000 issue of *The Journal of Affective Disorders*, researchers interview 20 people like Moore (not his real name) whose lives had been disrupted by the Internet. Nearly all of them were diagnosed with serious mental illness such as bipolar disorder. Many were sacrificing sleep to spend an average of 30 hours a week online outside work.
>
> https://www.cs.oberlin.edu/~btaitelb/addiction/wordeffects.htm

Since the Internet is such a powerful multimedia experience, one may become desensitized to less stimulating modalities, such as reading. Attention and concentration-span can decrease as a result of depression.

DOI: 10.1057/9781137565457.0008

The Internet of things

This notion involves tying all the objects and people in the world to everything else with tiny identifying devices such as Radio Frequency Identification (RFID) devices. This means that the Internet can keep tabs on everyone and everything—which may be useful as far as businesses knowing how much of everything they have and marketing but has ominous implications as far as human freedom is concerned. Theorists predict that by 2020 there will be more than 25 billion devices connected to one another.

As a curious example of how the Internet is insinuating itself into every aspect of daily life, consider the new Internet toothbrushes. They enable people brushing their teeth with these devices to obtain accurate information on how long they've brushed their teeth and other data about their teeth. An article by Sam Schechner in *The Wall Street Journal*, "Web-Enabled Toothbrushes Join the Internet of Things" describes these devices:

> BARCELONA—What the world needs now is a Web-enabled toothbrush. That part is clear to several oral-hygiene companies. What they can't agree on is who was first to put teeth into the smartphone. The giant Procter & Gamble Co. PG + 1.30% last week demonstrated what it calls the "World's First Available Interactive Electric Toothbrush." It links with a smartphone and records brushing habits, while an app gives mouth-care tips alongside news headlines. French startup bristles at that claim. Paris-based Kolbe also last week touted the "World's First Connected Electric Toothbrush."
>
> Gigahttp://online.wsj.com/news/articles/SB10001424052702304360704 579415161522531046?mg=reno64-wsj&url=http%3A%2F%2Fonline.wsj. com%2Farticle%2FSB10m.

Kolbe argues that it showed its toothbrush, which records dental data, in January, and thus should be considered to have created the first electronic toothbrush. Other new digital products have been created, such as smart socks, which track running form, and digital water bottles that keep records of water consumptions.

We can see that there's no end of things that can be tied to the Internet and it is reasonable to assume that someday everyone will have electronic chips planted in their bodies, which monitor all their bodily functions and send messages to doctors and others—such as the NSA or some other governmental entity—about where we are and the way our bodies are functioning and any physical or emotional problems we

DOI: 10.1057/9781137565457.0008

may be having. It is possible, in the Internet of things, that we will arrive at a state in which everything will be connected to everything else but nobody will be talking to anyone else.

If you are interested in the social, psychological, and cultural impact of the Internet, you should sign up for reports from the Pew Internet Project. It conducts surveys and other research on various aspects of the Internet and sends reports about its findings. You can access it at: www. PewInternet.org. It supplies free data, infographics, and analysis of such topics as mobile technology, social networking, health, and library use. Here's a sample of a typical Pew Internet newsletter, written by Professor John Mariani of Syracuse University. jmariani@syracuse.com

> Twenty-five years after the World Wide Web was conceived, seven out every eight U.S. adults are on the internet and 90 percent of them say that's a good thing. Those were among the finds of a survey of 1,006 Americans 18 and older conducted in January by the Pew Research Internet Project as the World Wide Web's silver anniversary approached. The technology's birthday is reckoned as March 12, 1989, the date that Sir Tim Berners-Lee wrote a paper proposing a system for managing information on the internet that would become the framework for the Web. He released the code for the system for free on Christmas Day the following year. The Web made it easy for ordinary users to pull documents from the internet and to use it to interact with others. In 1995, only 14 percent of American adults were using the internet, according to previous Pew research. That exploded to 87 percent in Pew's latest survey. The trend is similar for broadband use, which is nearly universal today. The adoption story itself is amazing and hardly ever duplicated in world history. "Technology has not deployed this fast, ever," Lee Rainie, the director of Pew's Internet Project, told NPR. Adoption has been strongest among those best able to afford it. Pew found 99 percent of households earning more than $75,000 a year were using the internet. Young adults between 18 and 29 and respondents with college diplomas also were big adopters, with 97 percent of each group online. As the Web blossomed, so did the use of tools with which to access it. When Pew asked in 2000, 53 percent of the adult Americans surveyed said they owned cellphones. That percentage rose to 90 percent in the latest poll.

The Pew Report indicates that 58% of people now use smartphones, as compared with 35% in 2011 and a large percentage of internet users, more than two-thirds, use smartphones to access the Internet. The Pew Internet Newsletters are extremely useful and provide data-rich information about the impact of the Internet on American culture and society, and devices that we use to access it.

DOI: 10.1057/9781137565457.0008

Meanwhile, the Internet continues to play an important role in the lives of billions of people, all over the world. It is used by farmers in India, who have bypassed land-based phones and now use inexpensive cell phones to find out what they should charge for what they grow, and thanks to Twitter, it is used by people planning protests in many countries. That explains why one of the first thing dictators do is cut off their people's ability to use the Internet. There is now a program in which smartphones set up their own networks without using the Internet to counter the problems groups face when the Internet is closed down by dictators or governmental authorities (as in Hong Kong) to prevent protests.

DOI: 10.1057/9781137565457.0008

2

Smartphones: *Everyone Can Do Anything*

Abstract: *The smartphone is, many suggest, a revolutionary device that has changed the world—especially the Apple iPhone, which is the most important smartphone. There are, it turns out, more than 2500 different models of smartphones, 2 millions apps that can be used on them, and almost 7 billion smartphones in use. A new development in smartphone design, the phablet, which is a large smartphone that is also around the same size as a small tablet, is discussed. Then the idea of psychoanalyst Erik Erikson are used to help explain why smartphones play such an important role in the lives of teenagers. This is followed by a discussion of some of the negative effects of smartphone use and the desire, many smartphone users have, to wait for "the next big thing" in smartphones before upgrading to new smartphones.*

Berger, Arthur Asa. *Gizmos or: The Electronic Imperative: How Digital Devices have Transformed American Character and Culture*. New York: Palgrave Macmillan, 2015. DOI: 10.1057/9781137565457.0009.

We learn from the Bible that in the beginning (whenever that was) was the word.

> In the beginning was the Word, and the Word was with God, and the Word was God. The same was in the beginning with God. All things were made by him. (John 1:1–3)

And the word was spoken by someone to someone else in a conversation or someone in close proximity. Then came the telephone, which meant we could speak with people anywhere in the world. Later we developed cell phones, which means we no longer had to rely on so-called land phones in our houses or buildings but could talk to people from just about anywhere, as long as certain technical requisites were taken care of—generally by phone companies. Then came the iPhone, the first important smartphone, and the world changed. The *PC Magazine Encyclopedia* offers this description of the functionality of smartphones:

> A cellular telephone with built-in applications and Internet access. In addition to digital voice service, modern smartphones provide text messaging, e-mail, Web browsing, still and video cameras, MP3 player and video playback and calling. In addition to their built-in functions, smartphones run myriad free and paid applications, turning the once single-minded cellphone into a mobile personal computer....
>
> In 1994, IBM and BellSouth introduced a combination phone and PDA called the Simon Personal Communicator. Often touted as the first smartphone, Simon was costly and heavy (see personal communicator). It took another decade before smartphones became small and powerful enough to be widely used. Introduced in 2002, and due to its focus on e-mail, the BlackBerry became the popular, corporate smartphone, amassing a huge audience over the years. In 2007, the iPhone changed the industry forever.

An article on the Internet by Quentin Hardy that appeared on the *New York Times* "Bits" column (March 27, 2014), "Smartphones, The Disappointing Miracle," informs us that there are 2,582 models of smartphones, 691 carriers of mobile messages, 106 operating systems, and around 2 million apps. In short, there are a bewildering number of choices when it comes to choosing phones and deciding what apps to use on them (Figure 2.1).

DOI: 10.1057/9781137565457.0009

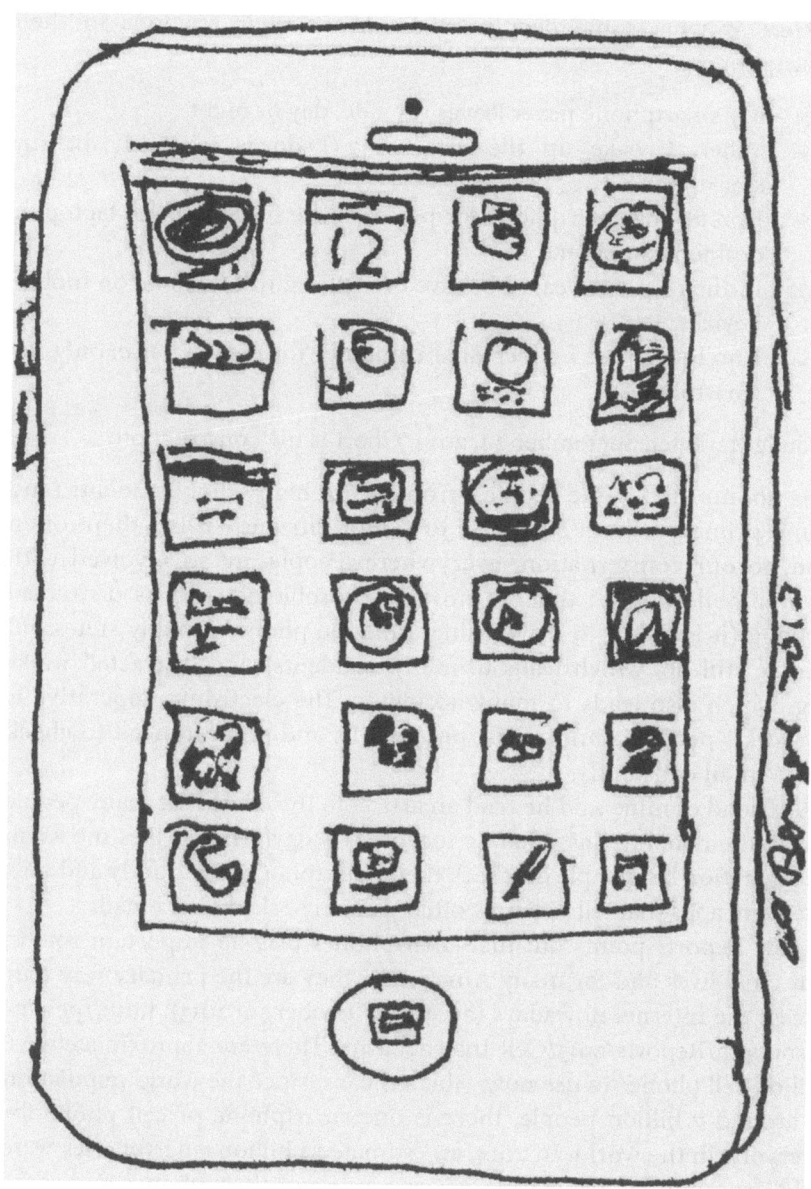

FIGURE 2.1   *Smartphone*

DOI: 10.1057/9781137565457.0009

Here is what some people tell us about their relations to their smartphones:

87%   My smartphone never leaves my side, day or night.

80%   When I wake up the first thing I do is to reach for my smartphone.

68%   I prefer my smartphone for personal use instead of my laptop or desktop computer.

60%   In the next five years I believe everything will be done on mobile devices.

34%   I no longer use my personal computer for personal use, only my smartphone

From eMarketer. September 24, 2014. Chart is my construction.

It is not unusual to see people—from junior high school students (and some primary school students) to senior citizens—using them often and, to our consternation, everywhere. People are so involved with their mobile phones that we now have problems such as distracted driving (it is illegal to drive using a mobile phone in many states but people still do, which leads to many accidents) and distracted walking, which also leads to many accidents. The electronic imperative is at work—people cannot resist phone calls and seem to need to check their email constantly.

A friend of mine said he read an article to the effect that many people check their mobiles as often as 100 times a day! That strikes me as an exaggeration but people do check their smartphones constantly and now there are apps that tell you how often you've checked your email.

Pew Reports points out that smartphones play an important role in our daily lives and for many Americans, they are the primary way they access the Internet nowadays (accessed October 16, 2013): http://pewinternet.org/Reports/2013/Cell-Internet.aspx. There are approximately 6.8 billion cell phones in use now, which means, since the world population is around 7 billion people, there is one smartphone or cell phone for everyone in the world. In 2014, an estimated 1 billion smartphones were sold—some to people getting newer models of their phones and some to people obtaining a smartphone for the first time. In some countries, such as the UK, Italy, and Sweden, mobile phone penetration is greater than 100%, which means just about everyone capable of using a mobile

DOI: 10.1057/9781137565457.0009

phone has one, and some people have more than one phone. As technology evolves, more people are buying smartphones to replace their less evolved cell phones. There are now curved smartphones and very large smartphones called Phablets, which represent a combination of smartphone and tablet. Apple's 6 Plus iPhone is a phablet. *Consumer Reports* now suggests that the Apple smartphones are the most technologically advanced phones available. We read:

> Apple's smartphones have gone through years of conservative, incremental updates, but the Apple iPhone 6 and 6 Plus catch up to and even surpass technically advanced Android rivals from Samsung, LG, and others. Let's start with what gets fixed with the Apple iPhone 6 and 6 Plus. The revamping includes a larger 4.7-inch screen for the iPhone 6 and a 5.5-inch one for the iPhone 6 Plus. Both phones, which are less than a quarter-inch thick, have the A8 processor that Apple claims is 25% faster than the iPhone 5s' already-fast A7 processor. This tweak, and their larger size, could help the Apple iPhone 6 and 6 Plus address a longtime iPhone weak spot: battery life. The other big news along with the new Apple Watch is a new mobile payment system called Apple Pay.

I might say that we don't know how long Apple's lead in smartphone technology will last because Samsung and other phone companies have just brought their smartphones to the marketplace and the ratings may change. Shortly after the introduction of the new iPhones in September 2014, I read a review of the new Samsung smartphone that said it was superior to the iPhone 6 Plus. So ratings are always changing. But having high ratings from *Consumer Reports* carries a lot of weight because they don't accept advertising and so their ratings are not biased in any way. On the other hand, they have been criticized for "loving" Apple products too much.

For many people it would seem that these phones are often used to assuage a kind of loneliness they feel, and using them can be seen as an attempt to deal with a feeling of alienation and a sense of isolation—a consequence, some would say, of the modern world and technology that both empowers us and, at the same time, alienates us. Marxists would say that these feelings are a result of the bourgeois capitalist society we all live in that generates this alienation in everyone. Freudians would say that smartphone use is a reflection of our unconscious needs for affiliation and affection and play a role in our development of an identity.

DOI: 10.1057/9781137565457.0009

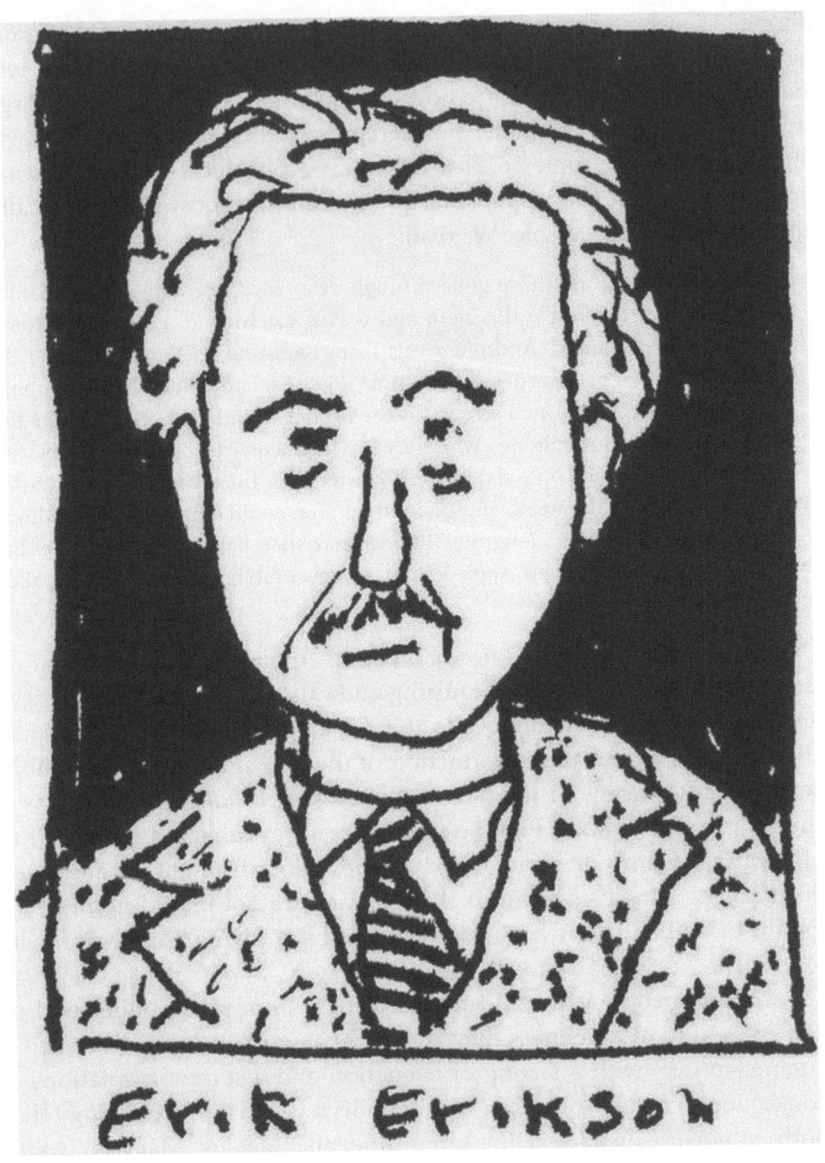

FIGURE 2.2   *Erik Erikson*

DOI: 10.1057/9781137565457.0009

A psychoanalytic perspective on mobile phones and adolescence

A psychoanalyst named Erik Erikson, has ideas about human development that can help us understand the role that smartphones play in our lives. His book, *Childhood and Society* (1963) argues as people grow older, they face eight crises, at different stages in their lives. Erikson's crises, which all take the form of polar oppositions, are listed below, along with suggestions about the roles that smartphones play relative to these crises. We find this material on the eight crises in his chapter on "The Eight States of Man" in *Childhood and Society.* I have eliminated the first two stages since it deals with infants and children too young to use smartphones, though they may play with them.

Erikson argues that we all face a number of crises and have to figure out a way to deal with them successfully as we move from infancy to old age. His analysis of adolescence and its crisis of "Identity and Role Confusion" is helpful in understanding smartphone use by young people. Adolescents, he argues, are disturbed by the problems they face relative to finding an occupation and, at that stage, tend to over-identify with heroes and celebrities of one kind or another. They seek to firm up their identities through communications they have with others and with love partners. As he writes (1963):

> To a considerable extent adolescent love is an attempt to arrive at a definition of one's identity by projecting one's diffused ego image on another and by seeing it thus reflected and gradually clarified. This is why so much of young love is conversation. (p. 261)

This helps explain countless text messages young people send one another. These messages are significant because they play an important role in attempts at self-definition by adolescents.

TABLE 2.1   *Psychological crises and the smartphone*

Stage	Crisis	Smartphone functions
Childhood	Initiative/Guilt	Family Integration, Play, Amusement
School	Industry/Inferiority	Socialization, Schoolwork Skills
Adolescence	Identity/Role Confusion	Peer Group Bonding, Schoolwork, Romance
Young Adult	Intimacy/Isolation	Love, Career Initiation
Adult	Generativity/Stagnation	Career, Community
Maturity	Ego Integrity/Despair	Contact, Community

DOI: 10.1057/9781137565457.0009

David Brooks, a columnist for *The New York Times*, wrote an interesting column, "Lord of the Memes," which deals with changes that have taken place in what might be called "intellectual affectation" (August 8, 2008, A19). There have been, he suggests, three epochs of importance. The first, from 1400 to 1965 was one of snobbery, in which there was a hierarchy of cultural artifacts with works from the fine arts and opera at the highest level and the strip tease at the lowest level. In the 1960s, he writes, high modernism was in vogue.

In the late 1960s this snobbery epoch was replaced by what he calls the "Higher Eclectica." This epoch was characterized by dumping the arts (generally speaking, the elite arts such as opera, ballet, classical music, etc.) valued in the epoch of snobbery in favor of a mixture of arts created by members of "colonially oppressed out-groups." What he is describing, though he doesn't mention it, is the impact of postmodernism upon culture, with its emphasis on eclecticism and the pastiche. It was "cool" to have a record collection with all kinds of "world" music and to decorate your house with religious icons or totems from Africa or Thailand.

"But on or about June 29, 2007, human character changed," Brooks writes. That was when the first iPhone was released. [He may have been reading Virginia Woolf before making that assertion.] On that date, Brooks asserts, "media displaced culture." What he means is that the way we transmit things, using media, replaced the content of what we create, culture. Really hip and cool people can be recognized as such because they are both early adopters and early discarders of the newest gizmos. Brooks was writing a satirical article, but his notion that American culture really changed when the iPhone was introduced isn't too far-fetched. Having a mobile phone was of use to many supporters of the Democratic presidential nominee Barack Obama, for he indicated his choice of a Vice President by sending text messages and email messages to people who had registered their phones and email addresses with him before he announced his choice to the press.

Smartphones are popular because they are useful in so many different ways. For example, teenagers like them because they escape from surveillance of their calls by their parents. These phones play a role, then, in what psychologists call the separation and individuation process. Parents often give cell phones or smartphones to their young children in order to keep tabs on them and maintain contact with them wherever they are. The phones can function, we see, as a kind of electronic leash. Now we

DOI: 10.1057/9781137565457.0009

also have smart wristbands and smart watches that monitor our hearts and other bodily functions (Apple brought out a smart watch on Friday, April 24, 2015) and can alert us (and our doctors) when they sense some kind of a problem. We can say that on that day our wrists started being colonized by Apple.

Negative effects of mobile phone usage

There are many negative aspects to the widespread use of smartphones and cell phones in general, which often are a big public nuisance, since people with mobile phones sometimes have loud conversations in public places, where they disturb others near them. It is possible that some airline companies in America may enable passengers to use their smartphones during flights. As you can imagine, this idea has generated a great deal of controversy. Spending hours on a flight sitting next to a person chatting on a cell phone is not appealing to most people.

Prior to the release of the first iPhone there was a widespread hysteria among Apple fans, and some Apple fans actually camped out on sidewalks in front of Apple Stores so they could be among the first to get the phones. Every year, it seems, Apple releases a newer, more powerful iPhone with expanded features, but so do other manufacturers such as Google, Samsung, Motorola, HTC, and LG. Despite all the competition, the iPhone has been an enormous success and has become a cultural icon. The iPhone is the source of most of Apple's profits—due to its very high margins—and some market researchers worry that if, for some reason, the iPhones lose their popularity, Apple will be in big trouble.

We might ask ourselves this question: why do people spend so much time on their smartphones? Do they use them to make calls they need to make or use them because they have them at their disposal and want to use them because they are lonely and feel the desire to speak with someone—maybe anyone? For some people, these phones free them from having to stay in offices to conduct business. They have help blur the distinction between work and play since, thanks to these phones, it is possible to do both at the same time. These phones have also blurred the difference between private and public, with many users conducting private conversations in public places—often with loud voices, disturbing others and forcing them to imagine what is being said by the person on the other end of the call.

DOI: 10.1057/9781137565457.0009

It may be that we are all so pressed for time nowadays that we have to multitask, so using smartphones becomes an indicator of a level of widespread cultural stress. Marxists might see cell phone use as reflecting the alienation and loneliness people feel in bourgeois capitalist countries, where classes are pitted against one another and people are susceptible to advertisements and social pressures that convince them that they must own smartphones. These phones also have revolutionary aspects, enabling people to form flash mobs and fight against dictatorial regimes.

Spencer A. Ante wrote an article titled "Smartphone Upgrades Slow as the 'Wow' Factor Fades" in the July 17, 2013 *Wall Street Journal* (page B1), which suggests that our fascination with new smartphones may be fading a bit. Ante points out that since we now have 70% of contract subscribers with smartphones, there are fewer people available to upgrade to smartphone usage and data plans and the changes to smartphones have been relatively modest, so users are not as tempted to upgrade as frequently as they did in the past years. Thus, many smartphone users stick with the phones they've been using while they wait for "the next big thing" in smartphones to be created. In addition, now some phone plans allow smartphone users to change their phones whenever they want, without penalties, instead of having to wait for two years.

When Apple introduced two iPhones in September, 2014 it sold 10 million smartphones over the weekend and approximately 40 million phones in the months that followed. So our passion for iPhones and other brands of smartphones, such as those made by Samsung (which now sells more smartphones than Apple does) continues, even though it may not be as feverish as it was in recent years. In January of 2014, Google sold Motorola, which it had purchased for 12 billion dollars, to Lenovo, a Chinese company, for around 2 billion dollars, which means Google lost 10 billion dollars on its Motorola smartphone adventure. What we learn from this is that there are huge profits and enormous dangers involved in manufacturing and selling smartphones. But "mobile" is now the center of advertising interest and will continue to be the most important, the most useful (with millions of apps) and the most powerful gizmo we use on a daily basis.

A carpenter who did some work for me recently is like many people nowadays who does not have a landline. I asked him for his email address and he gave it to me. When he told me he doesn't have a landline or a computer I asked him how he got his email. "On my iPhone," he said.

DOI: 10.1057/9781137565457.0009

"It's a computer." So he doesn't have a landline phone or a computer and is able to function with just a smartphone. That is the new world that we live in. The smartphone is the most revolutionary gizmo we've created and is magical in that it can do an incredible number of remarkable things—each of which is represented by an App. There are now millions of apps, which is a testimonial to human inventiveness, though they tend to cluster in certain areas: productivity, games, health monitoring, and so on.

Every day there is a new app representing some kind of technological breakthrough, so in the age of the smartphone, life is always exciting. You can now get apps that monitor how much time you spend on your smartphone or count the number of times you turn it on each day. These statistics, it is suggested, will make you realize how much time you are spending with your Smartphone and how dependent upon it you have become. This information can help you learn to spend less time using the smartphone and access it fewer times.

Note: This chapter is an updated, revised, and enhanced version of a chapter I wrote on Smartphones in my book *What Objects Mean: An Introduction to Material Culture*, published by the Left Coast Press.

DOI: 10.1057/9781137565457.0009

3
Television: *Everyone's Watching*

Abstract: *This chapter discusses television, the "medium we love to hate." It provides information on different kinds of television sets and what they cost. It discusses the important role narratives play in television programs and focuses on the Olympics and the role of sports in capturing the kind of audiences companies that advertise on television want—males between 18 and 49. It also provides data on the amount of time people in different racial and ethnic groups spend watching television, the amount of violence found in television and the number of commercials to which an average American child is exposed. Finally it discusses new challenges to television and the matter of whether the television set has become an anachronism.*

Berger, Arthur Asa. *Gizmos or: The Electronic Imperative: How Digital Devices have Transformed American Character and Culture.* New York: Palgrave Macmillan, 2015.
DOI: 10.1057/9781137565457.0010.

DOI: 10.1057/9781137565457.0010

The size and technologies of the television sets we have play a role in shaping our experience of television. Seeing a football game on a 19-inch flat screen television set, which is about the smallest set made for general use now, is different from seeing it on a 46-inch set or a larger one. Currently LED sets are the most popular kinds of television sets made but there are many other kinds made. When I checked the BestBuy website a year ago I found (Table 3.1):

TABLE 3.1   *Kinds of television sets and their prices*

LED television sets	55 inches for $1,800
Plasma television sets	51 inches for $550
OLED television sets	55 inches for $3,500
4K television sets	55 inches for $2,800
Curved OLED television sets	65 inches for $2,800

There were sales of television sets on July 3, 2012 and the prices of television sets have gone down considerably. An advertisement by Video Only in the July 3, 2015 *San Francisco Chronicle* shows that a "famous brand" 55-inch LED TV cost $649 and a 55-inch 4K Ulta LG television set cost $1,099. A 65-inch 4K Ultra Sony cost $2,599. There were no plasma sets in the advertisement.

We can see that television technology has been evolving quite rapidly over the years and technology companies find ways to make images sharper and colors brighter. And now, it is possible to watch television on our smartphones, so television programs are always available to us. LED television uses LED to backlight screens, instead of fluorescent bulbs and are more popular than Plasma sets because they only come in large screen sizes—42 inches and larger. OLED stands for Organic Light Emitting Diodes and are much more expensive than LED sets. At Best Buy, a 55-inch LED television set costs around $1,800 and a 55-inch OLED set costs $3,300, almost twice as much. What we call 4K television is another name for Ultra High Definition television sets that display 3840 by 2160 pixels, which has approximately four times as many pixels as the display on LED sets with 1080 pixels resolution. There are also some inexpensive small televisions with 720 pixel resolutions. I recently purchased a small name brand 720 pixel set for my study for $79 at Best Buy.

Where one places one's largest screen television set is also an indicator of television's role in a family's entertainment life. Many people put their largest screen television set (or main set, since many families have more than one

DOI: 10.1057/9781137565457.0010

television) in their living rooms and have other, smaller sets in bedrooms and kitchens. If parents allow their children to have their own television set that is usually an indicator that these children will watch a great deal of television since their watching is not always monitored. Many psychologists suggest that children should not be allowed to have their own television sets and that the amount of time they are allowed to watch television should be limited to an hour a day, at the most. In some families, television is used as a babysitter and children are allowed to watch a great deal more television, which psychologists and pediatricians say is not good for them.

The medium we love to hate

Neil Postman, one of the most astute analysts of media and popular culture, believes—as the title of his book suggests, that we are "amusing ourselves to death." As he explains in his book *Amusing Ourselves to Death: Public Discourse in the Age of Show Business*:

> There is no more disturbing consequence of the electronic and graphic revolution than this: that the world as given to us through television seems natural, not bizarre. For the loss of the sense of the strange is a sign of adjustment, and the extent to which we have adjusted is a measure of the extent to which we have changed. Our culture's adjustment to the epistemology of television is by now almost complete; we have so thoroughly accepted its definitions of truth, knowledge and reality that irrelevance seems to us to be filled with import, and incoherence seems eminently sane.

Television is the medium we love to hate. It has been described as a "vast wasteland," and it is a wasteland, but there are also some excellent programs on television—everything from symphonic music, operas, and ballets on public television stations to dramas, sitcoms, and football games on commercial networks.

Most people in the United States still spend more than five hours a day watching television. In addition to watching over-the-air television shows, many people in the United States also have cable or direct TV, which means, depending upon what service they've purchased, they can access hundreds of channels at any given moment. And they can record programs they want to see on various kinds of digital recorders, which means that they can time shift and see programs they like whenever they want. In addition, they can avoid television commercials on these digital recorders, which means that companies that advertise on television have

DOI: 10.1057/9781137565457.0010

little certainty that audiences will see their commercials. Since the main attraction of television for advertisers is that it can (or could) attract audiences, the television industry is facing a crisis.

But television, despite all the problems it faces, remains the most important element in our media consumption and plays an important role in our consumer culture, as Tom Doctoroff, a prominent advertising executive, explains (LinkedIn Pulse, accessed July 2, 2015):

> First, when we shop, our brand preference is typically shaped by "traditional media," while our engagement and loyalty to a brand is more likely influenced by digital media. Despite the proliferation of smartphones and other digital devices, the 30-second broadcast television commercial continues to rule (and increase)—even in the United States. According to eMarketer.com, manufacturers spent some $70 billion on network and cable advertising in 2014, up from $64.5 billion in 2012. While this suggests that companies think television ads remain a wise investment, digital media is more likely to increase the probability of purchase and repurchases because it effectively triggers behavioral changes, such as learning more, using more, buying more, and advocating more.

Television, Doctoroff explains, often works in conjunction with digital media and facilitating the purchase of products and services.

Television is a medium full of dramas

In 1982, Martin Esslin, a very astute analyst of media, explained in his book, *The Age of Television*, that it is a medium that is full of dramas. He writes (1982: 7):

> On the most obvious level television is a dramatic medium employing plot, dialogue, character, gesture, costume—the whole panoply of dramatic means of expression....According to the 1980 edition of *The Media Book*, in the Spring of 1979 American men on average watched television for over 21 hours per week, while the average American woman's viewing time reached just over 25 hours per week. The time devoted by the average American adult male to watching dramatic material on television thus amounts to over 12 hours per week, while the average American woman sees almost 16 hours of drama on television each week. That means the average American adult sees the equivalent of *five to six full-length stage plays a week!*...Television is the most voyeuristic of all communication media, not only because it provides more material in an unending stream of images and in the form most universally acceptable to the total population, but also because it is the most intimate of the dramatic media. In the theater,

DOI: 10.1057/9781137565457.0010

the actors are relatively remote from the audience, and the dramatic occasion is public. In the cinema, also a public occasion gathering a large audience into a single room, the actors are nearer to the spectators than in the theater, but in close-ups they are larger than life. Television is seen at close range and in a more private context. The close-up of the television performer is on a scale that most nearly approximates direct human contact.

Esslin was writing about programs that were fictional dramas—shows like the ones you find on CBS on Sunday evening such as "The Good Wife" and "The Mentalist." Television is full of fictional dramatic genres but it is possible to expand Esslin's definition of drama to include other areas. Thus, baseball games, football games, basketball games, hockey games, and so on, are essentially dramatic. So, in addition to seeing the equivalent of five or six full-length stage plays, we also spend a considerable amount of time watching exciting sports contests. If you watch any sports contests, you find that they are full of drama—often not being resolved until the last few seconds of a game. When you watch a televised game, in any sport, you often hear a collective gasp as a team wins a game with just a few seconds left. So television, I would suggest, is more dramatic that Esslin thought it was—but much of this drama is now found in sports contests. And it is sports that may save television as we know it. I'll say more about this shortly.

George Gerbner was dean of the Annenberg School of Communication at the University of Pennsylvania for many years. He developed a theory called "cultivation theory" that argued that television, the most dominant medium, gave many people distorted pictures of society. They thought that there was much more crime in the country than there was and that life was dangerous—because, he suggested, they got a false picture of life in America. That's because television has so many crime shows and the local news is full of reports on murders, shootings, fires, and so on.

Some critics of Gerbner's cultivation theory suggest that he doesn't consider the personalities and psyches of the people "cultivated" by television, who may have psychological problems that make them fearful—not the television programs they watch. Gerbner's theory also assumed that everyone more or less gets the same message from the programs they watch, a notion that is questionable in the views of many media researchers .

Many years ago, I attended a conference on television and the owner of a television station told me that if things work out the way they were going, network television would be dead in several decades. As I write this, in 2014, we've had the Super Bowl, watched by around 110 million people and when NBC showed the opening of the winter Olympics in

DOI: 10.1057/9781137565457.0010

Sochi, hundreds of millions of people all over the world watched it. In the United States, 34 million people watched the opening of the games, which is a very high number and a ratings success for NBC.

The television industry has a problem in that there are so many different channels and kinds of programs that the audience becomes split into many different segments—much like radio nowadays. But there are certain media events, such as the Super bowl or the Olympics, which attract enormous audiences and thus are of particular interest to advertisers. Curiously enough, the television commercials on the Super bowl are one of the main attractions of the event and people watch the commercials with interest, which makes advertising on the Super bowl very attractive to advertisers, even though commercials on the 2014 Super bowl cost 4 million dollars for 30 seconds. Television also commands large audiences when there are national tragedies or media events such as British royal marriages.

There are now a large number of special kinds of television shows—award programs such as the Clios or Emmies or Academy Awards that can attract a large audience, but even these shows cannot guarantee advertisers that people will watch the commercials shown during the ceremonies. And there are so many awards shows and they are so formulaic that many people have become turned off by the genre. In addition, cable companies are now supplying shows that, in many cases, are more interesting and more adventurous than broadcast television shows. So television has an existential threat from several sources: from shows produced on cable and from Digital Video Recorders that enable people to avoid watching commercials. There is also the matter of the time people spend on their mobiles that cuts into the amount of time they have available to watching television or listening to music or to the radio. Statistics show that young people now watch less television than they used to now that so many of them have smartphones.

Like all media, television has certain genres that it transmits, such as news, sports, crime dramas, detective stories, media events, situation comedies, comedy news shows, interview shows, talent shows (singing, dancing), and films, (which contain many of the same genres). To a considerable degree, television is a medium that carries narratives—stories of one kind or another, whether from real life or fictions. Esslin, in the quote at the beginning of this chapter, offered statistics for television viewing in 1979. Since then, we've watched more television than before, which means we are exposed to more dramas. As I explained earlier, I would also suggest that we broaden the term "narrative" to deal with

DOI: 10.1057/9781137565457.0010

any event—such as a football game or baseball game or an election—in which the outcome is not certain.

We can include reality contest television shows such as *American Idol,* (which was the dominant television show for eight years but is to be ended in 2016 after its ratings fell very low) and *Dancing With Stars,* which started in 2005 and remains popular. This show enables people to watch celebrities dance with professional dancers, and has clips of the celebrities rehearsing with the dancers and working hard to learn the routines. It combines celebrity watching with a contest, which generates dramatic excitement, since one team is eliminated every week until a winning team is declared. Reality television is very popular with audiences and with the producers of television shows since they don't have to pay writers to create scripts or actors and actresses. The drama in reality shows such as *Survivor* comes from the careful editing, which focuses upon conflicts and conspiracies among contestants and their teams (Figure 3.1).

The Olympics

That explains why the Olympics are so exciting to people. They cannot know, when a competition begins, who will win. Sports are a special

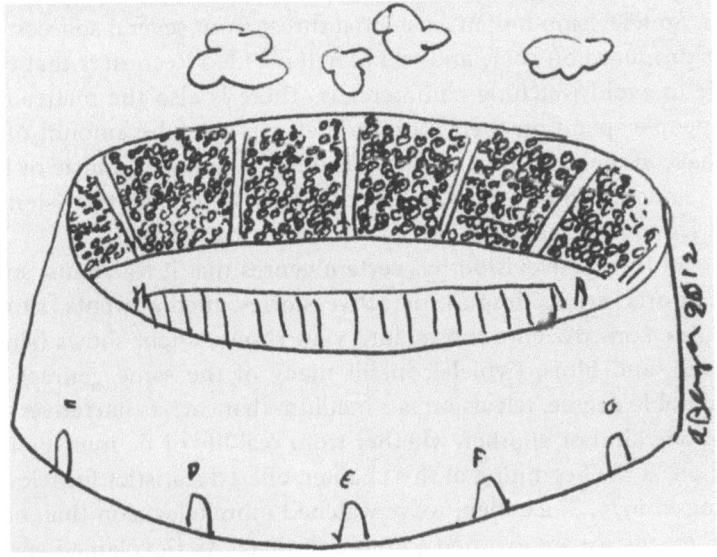

FIGURE 3.1   *Football stadium*

DOI: 10.1057/9781137565457.0010

form of drama that enable viewers to become emotionally involved in the contests—in part because there is so much information about the contestants. NBC enhances the dramatic quality of the contests by providing short biographies of many of the contestants, which enable people to identify with them emotionally. The Olympics also draw people together, for it enables people all over the world to share experiences together—even if NBC tapes the contests and broadcasts them at prime time in the United States. One thing about sports is that you don't have to know any languages to enjoy the spectacles of watching the finest athletes competing with one another.

There was also a subtext to the most recent Olympics, namely the political situation in Russia, the laws in Russia about homosexuals, the cost of the Olympics and the alleged cronyism that led to the cost ballooning to 50 billion dollars, and the danger from terrorists that everyone was conscious of and anxious about. In principle, the Olympics are supposed to bring people together, and they do, but there is also the element of nationalism as the competitions involve athletes from many different nations, each of whom is trying to maximize the number of medals they win. But the competitions are by individuals (or small groups, as is the case with hockey and ice skating) so their nationality plays an important role in the competitions but is not dominant. Individuals win or lose competitions but countries count up their medals.

One thing viewers learn from the games is that there are many accidents and chance events in each competition and losers generally take their defeats without sulking or being upset—for the most part. So losing is a major part of the Olympics experience. Most of the athletes at the Olympics do not believe that they will win a medal at all—but they are game to do the best they can, and there are always surprises. Sometimes the tension is enormous and the athletes find themselves enduring incredible pressure. In one dance competition, won by a Russian man and woman, after they finished dancing without making any major errors, the man collapsed on his knees and the woman started sobbing. They were so relieved from the stress they were under, representing their country (with the president of Russia, Vladimir Putin in the audience) that they collapsed. It is the way that television can transmit emotion that makes it such a powerful medium. There is also a lot of heartache in these games, as athletes lose some competition by a thousandth of a second or make some mistake and lose their chance at a gold medal or any kind of medal (Figure 3.2).

DOI: 10.1057/9781137565457.0010

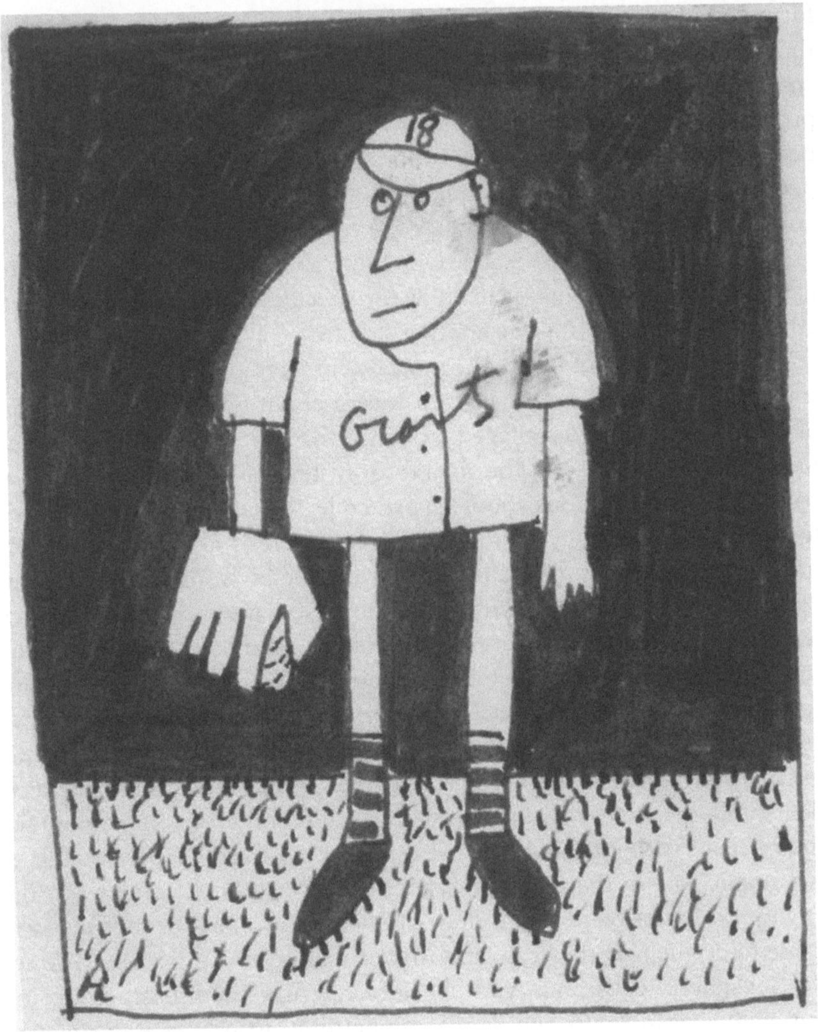

FIGURE 3.2   *Baseball player*

Sports to the rescue

As things stand now, football and other sports programs are preventing television in the United States from falling into a death spiral. People want to see football games, baseball games, and basketball games live, so these games are a kind of life raft that keeps broadcast television

DOI: 10.1057/9781137565457.0010

alive—along with certain comedy shows and various other feature programs. Football, especially professional football, provides advertisers with an audience they want to reach (males between eighteen and forty-five) who drink beer, buy automobiles, and do not time shift the games and delete the commercials on their digital video recorders. The current model in which companies pay to show commercials and networks survive on advertising revenue doesn't seem to be working very well and broadcast and cable television both need to find a better business model if they are to survive and prosper.

Below I offer some statistics on the use of television and family television statistics, which show that Americans spend a great deal of time watching television and that many Americans watch television while they are eating. Children, we find, are exposed to 16,000 television commercials each year, as well as countless acts of violence. Here are some statistics on television (the chart is my construction) that are of interest that add material to the statistics I presented earlier (Table 3.2):

TABLE 3.2   *Statistics on television viewing*

Average time spent in the USA watching television	5.11 hours per day
Hours spent by whites	5.02 hours per day
Hours spent by African Americans	7.12 hours per day
Hours spent by Hispanics	4.35 hours per day
Hours spent by Asians	3.14 hours per day
Years of life average person will spend watching television	9 years
Percentage of households with at least one television set	99%
Percentage of households with three or more TVs	65%
Percentage of Americans who regularly watch TV while eating dinner	67%
Number of hours per week the average child spends watching television	24
Number of thirty-second television commercials seen by average child in a year	16,000
Number of violent acts seen on television by age eighteen	150,000

These figures on television viewing in the United States show how large a role television viewing plays in our everyday lives. The typical American watches television for more than five hours, but more than 50% of Americans have cable and many watch programs on cable. It is broadcast television that is in trouble, especially now that cable networks are creating content—much of which, so critics suggest, is better than what the broadcast networks create. And many Americans watch sports on cable networks, such as ESPN. So, although Americans spend a great

DOI: 10.1057/9781137565457.0010

deal of time in front of their television sets, what they see on those sets is not always broadcast television. But the cable industry is also in trouble as more and more people drop the cable services, which average around $75 a month but can be substantially higher, depending upon the stations one signs up for.

Now there are devices such as Roku and Google's 35 dollar Chromecast that give viewers many choices when it comes to watching programs traditionally carried only by television. It is possible to see these new gizmos as stalking horses for an eventual move of television to the Internet, where people all over the world can watch what they want to see when they want to see it. It is generally recognized now that the Internet is the most important pipe into our homes and it is control of the Internet that will be the next battle among communication industries and the subject of regulation by the government. That, in fact, is the subject of Ken Auletta's article, "Outside the Box." Who controls what we see on our television sets is now the subject of a battle whose outcome remains to be seen.

In an article in the May 25, 2015 issue of LinkedIn Pulse, "7 Deadly Sins: Where Hollywood is Wrong About the Future of TV," Liam Boluk writes about the first "Deadly Sins":

By the Time You're Ready for OTT, You've Already Been Supplanted

For years, executives at the major television networks have repeated the same refrain: "We're aware of the over-the-top and direct-to-consumer opportunities… When it makes [economic] sense, we'll do it." And to point, nearly every network has a team of analysts obsessing over statistics such as the number of US broadband homes or annual authenticated video streams—all in the hope of discovering when, exactly, is the "right time" to disrupt their current Pay TV model.

What makes this strategy so dangerous is its tunnel vision: Every network assumes that when the OTT economics finally "make sense," they'll be as relevant to their audiences as they are today (or, more accurately, as they were yesterday). While Big TV waits, the major digital video providers and platforms will continue developing deep, routine and lucrative audience relationships. By the end of the decade, many traditional networks will be shocked to find they've been supplanted in the minds of many Millennials and Generation Zs. But this should come as no surprise.

What television will look like, and how people will access the kind of programs currently seen on television, remains a mystery. But the trends do not look promising for television's growth, since many Millennials

DOI: 10.1057/9781137565457.0010

(and others as well) now get their "television" shows on the Internet. Recent statistics suggest that half of the Millennials do not watch television on television sets but, instead, on devices that enable them to steam the content they wish.

Ken Auletta offered an assessment of the problems the television industry faces in an article in *The New Yorker,* "Outside the Box: Netflix and the Future of Television" (*The New Yorker,* February 3, 2014):

> Today, the audience for the broadcast networks is a third of what it was in the late seventies, lost to a proliferating array of viewing options. First came cable-television networks, which delivered HBO, ESPN, CNN, Nickelodeon, and dozens of other channels through a coaxial cable. Cable operators and networks charged monthly fees and sold ads, and even commercial-free premium networks such as HBO made money for cable operators because they attracted subscribers.... The advent of the Internet and streaming video brought new competitors.

Not only is television having problems—though it remains the device we use for most of our digital entertainment needs—but the television set may be an anachronism.

An article by Alex Williams in the November 7, 2014 issue of the *New York Times* explains that the television set may have outlived its usefulness. He writes, in an article titled "For Millennials, The End of the TV Viewing Party":

> Just as the landline went from household staple to quaint anachronism seemingly overnight during the last decade (acquiring a profoundly uncool air along the way), the television set has started to look at best like a luxury, if not an irrelevance, in the eyes of many members of the wired generation, who have moved past the "cord-cutter" stage, in which they get rid of cable, to getting rid of their TV sets entirely.

Research conducted by the Consumer Electronics Association offers more information on the shift by Millennials (those born after 1980) from "Appointment" television watching to "on-demand" television and video watching:

> According to the preliminary results of the second **NATPE||Content First** and the **Consumer Electronics Association** CEA)' joint research study on consumers' attitudes toward television viewing, just 55% of millennials use TVs as their primary viewing platform, while streaming devices— laptops, tablets, and smartphones—are poised to dominate their viewing preferences.

DOI: 10.1057/9781137565457.0010

So the television set may be one gizmo that is losing its importance, even though watching television shows and videos remains popular with Millennials and others. They use the Internet and have ditched their television sets.

DOI: 10.1057/9781137565457.0010

4
Tablet Computers:
Everyone's a God

Abstract: *It was the introduction of the iPad in 2010 that made the tablet an important new consumer device and now 10 inch and smaller 7 inch tablets are very popular, though the sales of tablets peaked in 2014. An article by Steven Levy suggests that the tablet represents an important rethinking of how people use computers—clicking on icons rather than on programs—and is designed for media consumption, reading, and gaming. Microsoft introduced a tablet in 2002 but it used a computer's operating system that was large and expensive. A fanciful analysis of tablets as they relate to myths is offered and the popularity of tablets is connected to certain imperatives in the collective consumer unconscious. The tablet is an important example of a product that people didn't know they wanted until they could get them.*

Berger, Arthur Asa. *Gizmos or: The Electronic Imperative: How Digital Devices have Transformed American Character and Culture.* New York: Palgrave Macmillan, 2015.
DOI: 10.1057/9781137565457.0011.

Recently, at a supermarket, I noticed a woman of about fifty who was shopping and was carrying a 7 inch tablet on which she had posted her shopping list. "That's interesting," I thought. "She can bring the store's ad—sent out every week on the Internet—along with a list of whatever it is she might wish to buy and any coupons that are available, as well." This story suggests the degree to which tablets have become part of everyday life for many people.

But what is a tablet? A Wikipedia article offers us a comprehensive understanding of what tablets are and how they have evolved.

> **Tablet computer**, or simply **tablet**, is a mobile computer with display, circuitry and battery in a single unit. Tablets are equipped with sensors, including cameras, microphone, accelerometer and touchscreen, with finger or stylus gestures replacing computer mouse and keyboard. Tablets may include physical buttons, for example, to control basic features such as speaker volume and power and ports for network communications and to charge the battery. An on-screen, pop up virtual keyboard is usually used for typing. Tablets are typically larger than smartphones or personal digital assistants at seven-inches (18 cm) or larger, measured diagonally. *Hybrids* that include detachable keyboards have been sold since the mid-1990s. Convertible touchscreen notebook computers have an integrated keyboard that can be hidden by a swivel or slide joint. *Booklet* tablets have dual-touchscreens and can be used as a notebook by displaying a virtual keyboard on one of the displays. Conceptualized in the mid-20th century and prototyped and developed in the last two decades of that century, the devices became popular in 2010. As of March 2012, 31% of U.S. Internet users were reported to have a tablet, which was used mainly for viewing published content such as video and news. Among tablets available in 2012, the top-selling line of devices was Apple's iPad with 100 million sold by mid October 2012 since its release on April 3, 2010, followed by Amazon's Kindle Fire with 7 million, and Barnes & Noble's Nook with 5 million. As of May 2013, over 70% of mobile developers were targeting tablets (vs. 93% for smartphones and 18% for feature phones).

In recent years, the sale of tablets has diminished as they are being replaced, for many people, by phablets—that is phones with very large screens. I will say more about them later in the book.

The introduction of the iPad

When Steve Jobs introduced the iPad in 2010 many people considered it as not having much potential. Yet, as the Wikipedia selection below shows, they were wrong:

DOI: 10.1057/9781137565457.0011

The first iPad was released on April 3, 2010; the most recent iPad models, the iPad Air and second generation iPad Mini, were revealed on October 22, 2013 and went on sale November 1, 2013, and November 12, 2013, respectively. The user interface is built around the device's multi-touch screen, including a virtual keyboard. The iPad has built-in Wi-Fi and, on some models, cellular connectivity. There have been over 170 million iPads sold since its release in 2010 (as of October 2013).[5]

In addition, there are many millions of other tablets made by other manufacturers, which have been sold by companies that raced to imitate the original 10 inch iPad and the 7 inch iPad minis.

In 2014 the tablet craze peaked and sales of tablets are now going down, perhaps because hundreds of millions of people already have them. One reason the sale of tablets is going down is that they are being replaced by very large screen smartphones called "phablets" that combine large screens and phone capabilities. Even Apple is having trouble selling tablets now. The sales of Apple tablets declined somewhat in 2014. This decline raised an interesting question: has the public's appetite for tablets peaked or was the decline merely a "bump in the road."

In an article in *Wired*, "How the Tablet Will Change the World," Steven Levy explained the cultural significance of the iPad (March 22, 2010):

> Even though the iPad looks like an iPhone built for the supersize inhabitants of Pandora, its ambitions are as much about shrinking our laptops as about stretching our smartphones. Yes, the iPad is designed for reading, gaming, and media consumption. But it also represents an ambitious rethinking of how we use computers. No more files and folders, physical keyboards and mouses. Instead, the iPad offers a streamlined yet powerful intuitive experience that's psychically in tune with our mobile, attention-challenged, super-connected new century. Instant-on power. Lightning-fast multitouch response. Native applications downloaded from a single source that simplifies purchases, organizes updates, and ensures security.

So the iPad and all its competitors marked a revolutionary change in the way people interacted with computers—clicking on icons rather than programs, which is the way desktop and laptop computers work.

Two questions about computer tablets

Two questions demand attention, relative to tablets: the first is why are they so popular? and the second is why did it take so long to create a

DOI: 10.1057/9781137565457.0011

decent tablet? I said "decent" tablet because Microsoft came out with a tablet years ago in 2002 but it was large, not very functional, heavy, and expensive ($2,000) and had a computer's operating system. Very few people bought it and it more or less died from inattention. Steve Jobs had a different vision for tablets—as consumer devices with their own operating systems, that sold for much less than a desktop computer and had Apple's superior design elements.

The reason tablets are popular is because they are so functional. You can turn on your apps with a single click and you can check your email on them and type email messages more easily than on a smartphone, because the keys on tablet screens are much larger, so it is easier to type on tablets (at least in principle) than on mobiles. My wife finds typing emails on her smartphone very difficult and I have the same problem. On the other hand, many young people can type amazingly quickly, just using their thumbs, on their mobiles.

The new "micro" or 7 inch tablets are also very light and some of them, such as the Apple iPad mini and Google's Nexus 7 tablets, have screens with very high resolutions and brilliant colors. Google's advertisement for the Nexus 7 reads as follows:

> Now thinner, lighter, and faster—Nexus 7 brings you the perfect mix of power and portability and features the world's sharpest 7" tablet screen—putting over 2.3 million pixels in the palm of your hand.

> With 323 pixels packed into every inch, you can read text that's sharper than the printed word, see images more vivid than the highest quality photo magazine, and watch videos come to life in vibrant 1080p HD.

The Google Nexus 7 sells for $229 (though I bought one for my wife on Valentine's Day, 2014, for $199.95), a good deal less than the iPad mini with retina display. Many people who are Apple fans are willing to spend more money for their tablets because of their identification with the Apple brand and because of the high quality of Apple products. They are what we might describe as "brand advocates," whose loyalty to the Apple brand is very strong (Figures 4.1 and 4.2).

The "myth model" and tablets: A fanciful hypothesis

Anyone who has read the Bible must recall how tablets—stone, not electronic—played an important role in history. In the Old Testament we read about Moses going up on a mountain and staying there for forty

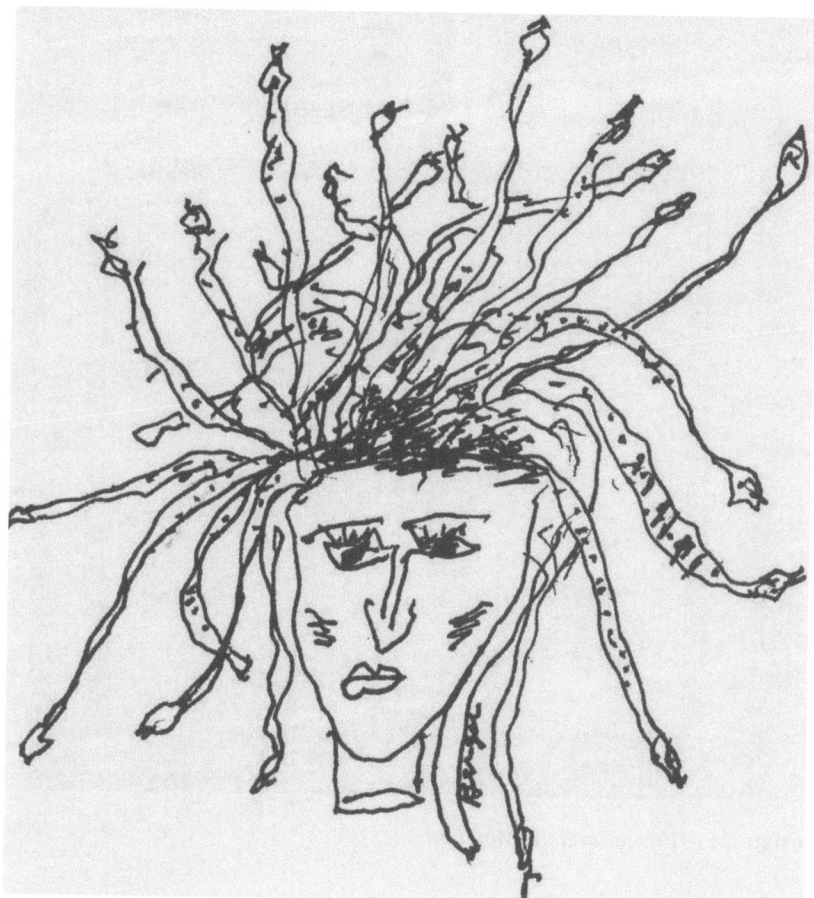

FIGURE 4.1   *Medusa*

days and forty nights. He comes down, with two tablets, bearing the ten commandments, but when he sees the Hebrews celebrating a Golden Calf they have made while he was away, he becomes angry and dashes the tablets to the ground, breaking them. Eventually he goes up on top of the mountain again and gets two more tablets, which he brings down to earth whole, and does not shatter them. This story from the Bible suggests that tablets, which contain texts of one kind or another, have an important role in the Western world and have had an impact on our collective imaginations. I should add that if these devices were called

DOI: 10.1057/9781137565457.0011

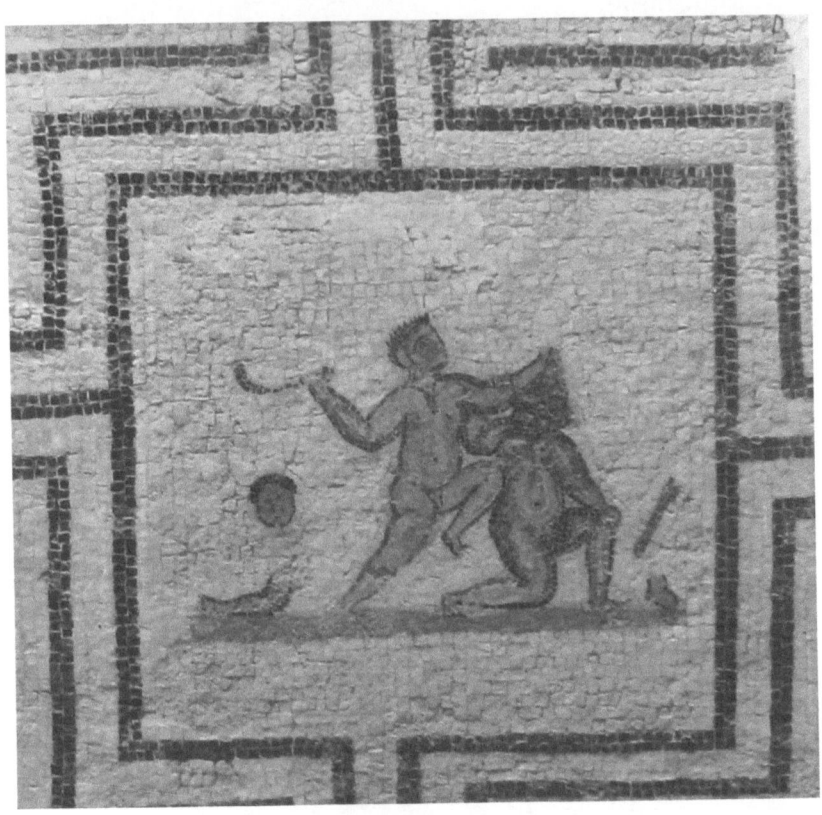

FIGURE 4.2   *Theseus and the Minotaur*

something like "slates" or something other than tablets, I would not be making this analysis.

Let me suggest, then, that in the Western world, our digital tablets are connected, in our collective psyches, to the Biblical story of Moses and his tablets. I am arguing, here, that myths shape many of our behaviors, even though we are not aware that this is the case. Around ten years ago I came to the conclusion that myths play an important role in our lives and developed a myth model that suggested, in essence, that many of the things we do are tied to ancient myths. Or to put in a different way, many of our activities can be seen as desacralized manifestations of ancient myths.

We can define myths as sacred stories, believed to be true, about the origins of life.

DOI: 10.1057/9781137565457.0011

Raphael Patai, a scholar of myth writes in his book *Myth and Modern Man* about myth (1972: 2):

> Myth…is a traditional religious charter, which operates by validating laws, customs, rites, institutions and beliefs, or explaining socio-cultural situations and natural phenomena, and taking the form of stories, believed to be true, about divine beings and heroes…Myths are dramatic stories that form a sacred charter either authorizing the continuance of ancient institutions, customs, rites and beliefs in the area where they are current, or approving alterations.

Patai adds that myths play an important role in shaping social life and writes that "myth not only validates or authorizes customs, rites, institutions, beliefs, and so forth, but frequently is directly responsible for creating them" (1972: 2).

Mircea Eliade, a scholar of religion, argues that we have emptied the religious content out of many myths and don't recognize that our behavior is often tied to some myth or myths. The myth model that I develop shows how ancient myths inform many contemporary activities. My myth model has a number of components: a myth, the way this myth can be found in history, psychoanalytic theories connected to this myth, its use in elite culture and popular culture texts (works) and its manifestation in everyday life. The myth I will use to help explain our attraction to and attachment to tablets is the myth of Moses, who is given two tablets on which God has written, destroys the tablets when he sees the Jews worshiping a Golden Calf they have made while Moses was away, for forty days and forty nights, on a mountain top.

In the passage of the Bible that deals with this topic, Moses has gone up on Mount Sinai for forty days and forty nights and is given two tablets. We read:

> When he finished speaking with him on Mount Sinai, He gave Moses the two Tablets of the Pact, stone tablets inscribed with the finger of God.

This material is found in The Jewish Publication Society of America's book *The Torah: The Five Books of Moses: A New Translation of The Holy Scriptures according to the Traditional Hebrew text.* This translation is more accurate, though less poetic, than the King James version. Another version of this story, from the Stone edition of the Torah (Mesorah Publications, 1997) follows:

> And he gave unto Moses, when he had made an end of communing with him upon Mount Sinai, two tablets of testimony, tablets of stone written with the finger of God.

DOI: 10.1057/9781137565457.0011

What we find here is that God is the first tablet writer. Conventionally it is understood that the tablets contained the ten commandments but in Jewish translations of the story, it is the Torah—the first five books of the Bible. We read (in the Stone edition of the Torah):

> And it came to pass as soon as he came nigh unto the camp that he saw the calf, and the dancing, and Moses's anger waxed hot, and he cast the tables out of his hand and broke them beneath the mount.

We take these events as the mythic element in the myth model. The way this model can be found in history and other aspects of our culture follows:

Myth	Moses and the Tablets with the Ten Commandments
Historical Act	Invention of Digital Tablet
Psychoanalytic Theory	Messianic Complex
Elite Culture Text	Statue of Moses by Michelangelo
Popular Culture Text	Political Cartoons of politicians with stone tablets
Everyday Life	Someone buys an iPad

I chose an iPad rather than another tablet because Apple's logo, which shows an apple with a bite out of it, is an allusion to Adam and Eve in the Garden of Eden. The bite suggests Adam or Eve took a bite from the apple on the tree of knowledge and because they disobeyed God, who told them they should not eat from the tree of knowledge, they learned that they were naked and were thrown out of the Garden of Eden. This connection between tablets and the story of Moses may help explain why one of the major Jewish websites is called "Tablet." It deals with Jewish news, politics, life, art, culture, and religion.

Now, as I pointed out earlier, there are devices called phablets that are very large smartphones that combine the size of the tablet and the functionality of the smartphone. These phablets typically have screens of 6 inches or more, which means they aren't as easy to carry around as regular smartphones, and different brands are designed for different kinds of users: game players, movie watchers, and so on. But they have very large screens and thus have the functionality of the smartphone and the tablet in one device. It's hard to know whether phablets are really small tablets that can make phone calls or phones with very large screens. They are very popular in Asian countries, where buyers want one device to take care of their phone calls and do things conventionally done on tablets. Phablets represent a kind of merging of two genres of gizmos in

DOI: 10.1057/9781137565457.0011

which we don't know where the phone ends and the tablet begins. Many devices now are like that. Phablets have become increasingly popular in the United States, where Apple finally decided to manufacture one, the Apple Plus, in 2014.

Tablets and the unconscious

I have tried to show in this discussion of tablets that our fascination with them may be tied to their mythic significance and is not just a matter of their functionality. Our gizmos often have roots in the sacred and are tied to areas of our psyches—what Freud called "the unconscious," of which we are unaware. That is what Ernest Dichter, the father of motivation research discovered, when he started investigating the way people felt about different products.

Earlier I discussed Gerald Zaltman's book, *How Customers Think: Essential Insights into the Mind of the Market*, which argues that there is a 95-5 split in our minds, with 95% of our cognition functioning below consciousness. Zaltman adds an important insight to this notion. He writes (2003: 51):

> *The 5% of our thinking that is highly conscious enables us to confront the 95% of mental life below this stratum.* We can contemplate what we are aware of, but many other elements are at work. Therefore, the managerial tendency to focus on conscious consumer thought, while understandable and natural, also blocks managers' access to the world of unconscious consumer thought and feeling that drives most consumer behavior.

Zaltman's discussion of the role of the consumer's unconscious may explain the significance of a statement by Steve Jobs that what he was interested in doing was creating products that we didn't know we needed or would want. The iPad was one of these products and the last new product that Apple created before its watch. What many people have been wondering now is what new product or service, that we don't know we need or want, will Apple come up with? The answer, we found out in 2015, was the Apple Smart Watch. But is it a product that people didn't know they need or want or that they don't need? That remains to be seen.

DOI: 10.1057/9781137565457.0011

5

Computers:
Everyone's a Writer

Abstract: *This chapter deals with computers, the device that really started the digital revolution. The famous 1984 Macintosh commercial is discussed, showing how it reflected ambivalent view we have about computers and their role in society and our lives. Computers play a major role in the development of our digital culture. The ability of computers to edit texts and images and films is dealt with. Next I offer statistics showing that the sale of desktop computers has peaked, though they still sell in huge numbers. This if followed by a discussion of the ability of computers to recognize faces and the existence of programs that can scan faces and obtain reliable information about our emotions as well as medical and psychological problems.*

Berger, Arthur Asa. *Gizmos or: The Electronic Imperative: How Digital Devices have Transformed American Character and Culture.* New York: Palgrave Macmillan, 2015.
DOI: 10.1057/9781137565457.0012.

DOI: 10.1057/9781137565457.0012

Legend has it that fifty years ago, when a vice president of some big electronic company was asked about how many computers might be sold, he replied that a dozen or so would probably be enough for the entire country. This was when computers were the size of a large room and cost a small fortune. He didn't recognize the appeal these gizmos had for people, for the computer and the Internet opened the world up in new ways. Janet H. Murray dealt with the potentialities of the computer in her book, *Hamlet on the Holodeck: The Future of Narrative in Cyberspace* (1997:84).

> Since every form of representation is migrating to electronic form and all the world's computers are potentially accessible to one another, we can now conceive of a single comprehensive global library of paintings, films, books, newspapers, television programs, and databases, a library that would be accessible from any point on the globe. It is as if the modern version of the great library of Alexandria, which contained all the knowledge of the ancient world, is about to rematerialize in the infinite expanses of cyberspace. Of course, the reality is much more chaotic and fragmented: networked information is often incomplete or misleading, search routines are often unbearably cumbersome and frustrating, and the information we desire seems to be tantalizingly out of reach. But when we turn our computer on and start up our Web browser, all the world's resources seem to be accessible, retrievable, immediate. It is a realm in which we can easily imagine ourselves to be omniscient.

What the computer could do for texts, which is Murray's focus, it soon will be able to do for things, when we have the Internet of Things—when every digital gizmo can be connected to every other one and controlled by our smartphones.

It was the personal computer that started the digital revolution as we know it. Once manufacturers learned how to make computers for a few thousand dollars, they became an essential part of many people's lives, and economies of scale have now led to very powerful personal computers being available for just a few hundred dollars. In the early 1980s I purchased a Commodore 64 for $600—for my son to play with and for me to use in word processing. The word processing on the Commodore 64 was very primitive but the important thing was I could write something and save it, and change what I'd written without having to retype the whole page or manuscript. Then I could print it out on a dot-matrix printer, another revolutionary device at the time (Figure 5.1).

The famous Macintosh "1984" commercial, directed by Ridley Scott, that introduced the Macintosh shows our ambivalence toward computers. The

DOI: 10.1057/9781137565457.0012

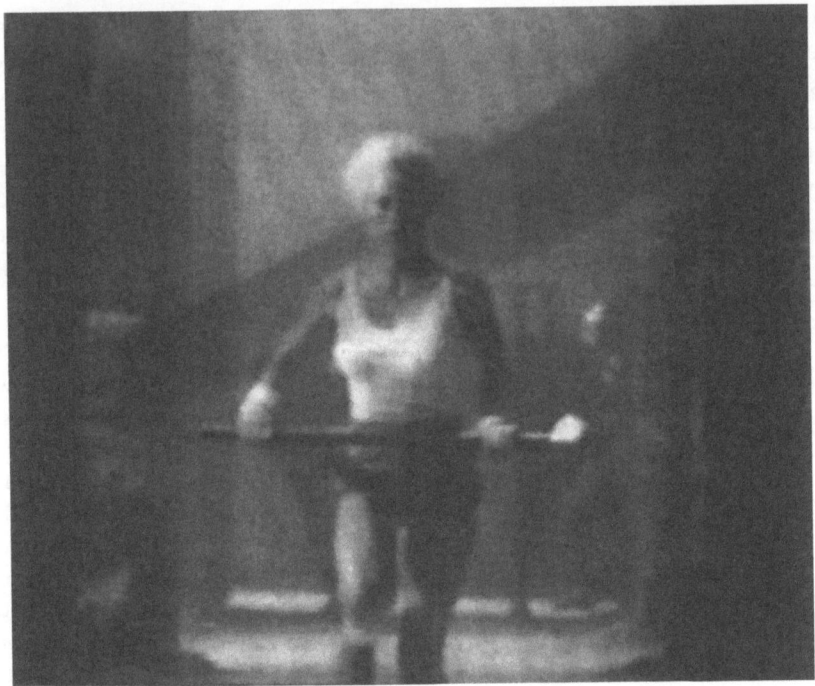

FIGURE 5.1   *Scene from Macintosh "1984" television commercial*

commercial featured a large group of skinheads with shaved heads who are shown as captives of some gigantic organization (read IBM here). They file into a huge auditorium and are being brainwashed by someone in that organization who is babbling nonsense. The Macintosh positioned itself as a means of helping people escape from what was portrayed as being enslaved (by IBM and non-Apple personal computers).

In the "1984" commercial, we see a beautiful blonde woman, clutching a large sledgehammer, being pursued by helmeted guards. She runs into the gigantic auditorium where the skinheads are being brainwashed and throws her sledgehammer at the screen. It explodes. This, we are led to understand, will help destroy the hold the brainwasher has on his victims, who stare, open-mouthed at what happens. The "1984" commercial is, perhaps, the most famous television commercial ever made. But it also reflects an ambivalence toward computers, which, we see, have the power to enslave us. The Apple icon of an apple with a bite out of it connects Apple's computers with the story of Adam and Eve in

DOI: 10.1057/9781137565457.0012

the Garden of Eden. The bite out of the apple reflects Adam and Eve's having eaten from the tree of knowledge that ultimately led to them being expelled from the Garden of Eden.

As a result of the files stolen by Edward Snowden from government computers and released by various publications, we know now that the American government has a huge spy apparatus that can record every phone call we make, capture our emails, and spy on us—as well as people in foreign countries. The government has huge supercomputers that do its dirty work, so I would imagine that we can read the famous "1984" commercial differently now—with the head of the NSA replacing the bureaucrat from IBM as the villain. We realize now that everything we do electronically can be monitored and saved. The only way we can transmit information without it being monitored is through snail mail, and maybe the NSA is monitoring it, as well (Figure 5.2).

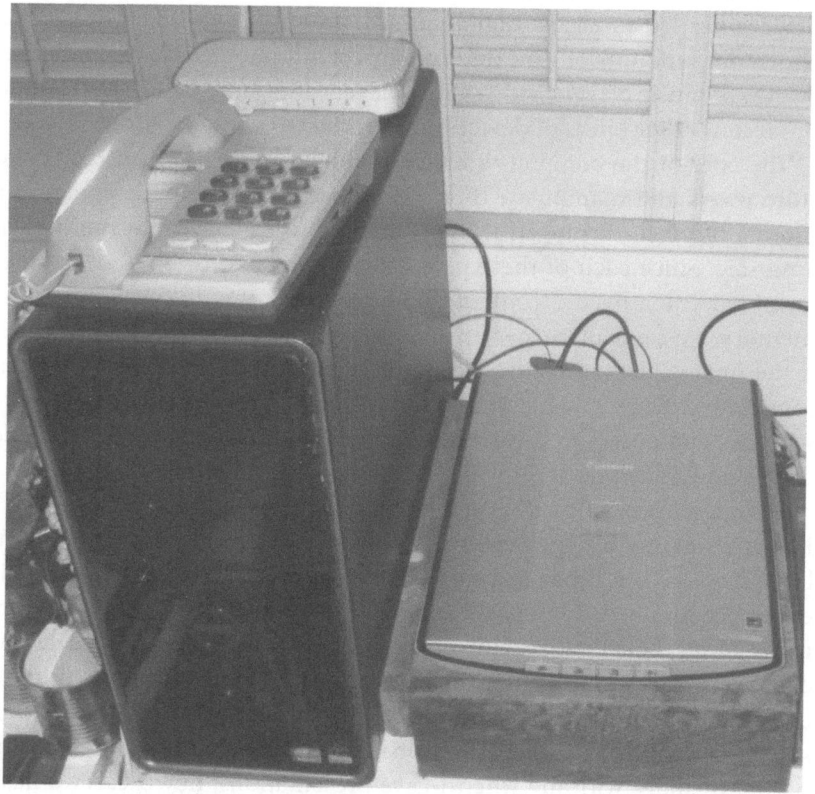

FIGURE 5.2   *My Dell computer and Canon scanner*

DOI: 10.1057/9781137565457.0012

In recent years, the price of entry-level desktop computers has fallen to around just a few hundred dollars and entry-level laptop computers are available for several hundred dollars. You can now (in 2015) get a Samsung Google Chrome book for around $250. Computers are digital devices that can perform manipulations and calculations at incredible speeds using a program, which can be defined as a stored set of instructions. It is useful, as computer technology has evolved, also to think of them as devices that can also manipulate and retrieve (on sites such as YouTube) visual data. It is possible now to edit films on computers. The most important symbols the computer can manipulate are *pixels* (pixel is short for "picture element" or, in essence, a dot), which can be used to create lines, shapes, and other visual phenomena.

It is the ability of computers and other digital devices to turn images into pixels that has been all important, for we can capture and manipulate these pixels as we wish. For Lunenfeld, the development of digital devices has led to a new digital culture—a culture in which we spend enormous amounts of time and money on cell phones, iPods, and other brands of music players, video game players and games, CDs, DVDs, and numerous other kinds of devices and products.

The core of the computer's image-making power lies in its ability to store pixels and manipulate them. What we call a computer image is a mosaic of pixels, arranged in rows and columns similar to the tiles in a mosaic. Since each of these pixels is assigned a location and a predetermined color by the computer, which stores this information in its memory, we can call images up and manipulate them in countless ways, if the image is being controlled by the right software. There have been remarkable developments in graphic software, which means that people who use computers to create and manipulate images can do incredible things nowadays.

Now, a genre of software designed for presentations, such as Microsoft's Power Point, enable speakers to display images and textual material on large screens. But it has to be used carefully, because members of audiences become bored if all speakers do show slides and read the textual material on their Power Point slides. Presentation software is extremely effective when speakers use images and other forms of infographics to communicate information and ideas. The development of presentation software has made the slide-show obsolete. I used to carry a large carousel full of slides with me when I gave presentations; now I carry a flash drive 2 inches long with forty presentations on it.

DOI: 10.1057/9781137565457.0012

With the development of powerful laptop computers, and tablet computers, the desktop computer is no longer the dominant kind of computer, but it retains its utility because it is possible to use a large monitor and the keyboards of desktops are easier to use than laptops. Many people have both, and now, thanks to cloud programs such as Google Drive, Microsoft One Drive, Amazon Cloud Drive, and Dropbox, people who bring their laptops to coffee houses to work can pick up on their desktops what they've done on their laptops. The chart below (my construction) shows the shipments of computers and other digital devices for 2013, 2014, and projected for 2015 and 2016. This chart, my construction, rounds off figures (Table 5.1).

TABLE 5.1   *Worldwide sales of computers, tablets, and mobile phones*

Device type	2013	2014	2015	2016
PC (Desk-based and Notebook)	303,000	281,000	259,000	248,000
Tablet	184,000	263,000	233,000	259,000
Mobile Phone	1,810,000	1,905,000	1,906,000	1,969,000
Total devices in billions	2.3	2.4	2.4	2.5

Note: Worldwide device shipments by segment (Thousands of units).
Source: Gartner, July 2015.

We see that the shipments of desktop computers is declining over the years, while the shipment of tablets is rising rapidly (though tablets seem to have peaked in 2014) and mobile phones is rising slowly. When you add up the figures for all these devices, you find that for 2015, something like 2.4 billion devices were shipped, which suggests that the computer, in its various forms and manifestations is now very widespread: there is one computer-like device for approximately every three people in the world.

One of the more interesting, and perhaps more ominous, developments using computers involves facial recognition software. In the Sochi Olympics, security officers are now using a facial recognition program that scans for minute, involuntary muscles flexing in people who may be terrorists. An article posted online by *The New Yorker* describes a new development in facial scanning, VibraImage:

> The Sochi Olympics, which face the gravest threat of terrorism of any Games in recent history, also host the event's most pervasive and expensive surveillance yet. The resort town's "ring of steel," as Russian officials have described it, consists of drones, soldiers, surveillance blimps, metal detectors, thousands

DOI: 10.1057/9781137565457.0012

of cameras, and other high-tech equipment, such as VibraImage, a scanning system that analyzes muscle vibrations in the neck and head to "detect someone who appears unremarkable but whose agitated mental state signals an imminent threat," reports the Times. Additionally, the registration process for the mandatory Olympics spectator badge is, in effect, a background check for every visitor.

February 14, 2014
Sochi's Other Legacy
Joshua Kopstein

The computer, we see, has unlimited capabilities; everything depends upon the software that is created for it. Facial scanning software can also detect physical ailments and mental problems.

According to Paul Ekman and Terrence J. Sejnowski (in their Executive Summary of report to National Science Foundation, downloaded from Internet), thanks to computers we now have automated systems for monitoring facial expressions and animating artificial models. Computers studying our facial expressions can provide information about our emotions and enduring moods (anger, fear, surprise, disgusts, sadness, etc.), our cognitive activity, our temperament and personality, our truthfulness (leakage of concealed emotions) and psychopathology (diagnostic information about depression, mania, schizophrenia, and less severe disorders), and applied medical research involving the role of emotions in coronary artery disease and other diseases. What's remarkable is that all of this kind of information derived from facial expression can be automated and done by computers. The Ekman and Sejnowski report was published in 2005. In the years since then, facial recognition software has made tremendous progress, as can be seen with the development of the VibraImage program and other similar programs.

The development of these powerful programs for recognizing emotions and other psychological phenomenon has implications as far as the role of governments in not only studying facial expression in people but also using this knowledge to control people. What happens when governments or social media (like Facebook) start using VibraImage programs and other like it on their own populations not only to study them but to control them? The supercomputers of the NSA, that can record phone calls and emails and God only knows what else, have made many Americans upset about the degree to which they are being monitored and the dangers that computers pose to our freedom.

DOI: 10.1057/9781137565457.0012

6

Video Game Consoles and Video Games: *Everyone's a Hero*

Abstract: *In this chapter I begin by offering a discussion of the role of video game consoles in the video game industry, the most important video game consoles, and the question of whether consoles will be supplanted by tablets and smartphones. Next I offer information on the most important kinds and genres of video games and statistics on the amount of money spent on handheld, mobile, personal computer, and video game consoles and a listing of the top ten video games of 2013. This is followed by a discussion of the attributes of video games, such as immersion and interactivity, and the problem of video game addiction. Finally I offer an analysis of PacMan as an example of how video games reflect important themes in American culture.*

Berger, Arthur Asa. Gizmos or: *The Electronic Imperative: How Digital Devices have Transformed American Character and Culture.* New York: Palgrave Macmillan, 2015. DOI: 10.1057/9781137565457.0013.

The Economic Times offers some statistics about the popularity of video games. In 2013, Microsoft and Sony introduced new video game consoles. Nintendo introduced its new console, the WiiU in 2012. Microsoft's Xbox One sells for $500 and the Sony PlayStation 4 sells for $400. Nintendo's Wii U, which has not been successful, sells for $300. In the United States, the Sony PlayStation is selling better than the Microsoft Xbox One for several reasons. First, it is $100 less expensive than the Xbox 1 and second, it is easier to use and doesn't require a complicated set up like the Xbox 1. As things stand now, Microsoft is waiting to see if a new videogame will lure gamers to its console. Great video games lead to the sales of the consoles on which they are played, so video game console makers have a big stake in attracting video game creators to their systems.

In his essay, "Video Games and the Emergence of Interactive Video," Eugene Provenzo explains that video games continue to evolve and become more powerful and involving—and violent. He writes:

> Each successive generation of video games has become more technologically sophisticated, more realistic, and more violent. The newest wave of video games, based on CD-ROM technology (the same technology people use for music recordings and computer software), is, in fact becoming more like film and television than what we traditionally expect of a video games. This is a major evolutionary step beyond the simple graphics of the classic *Space Invaders* arcade game so popular fifteen or twenty years ago, or the tiny animated cartoon figures of the Nintendo system that have dominated the video game market in recent years.

The irony, as I will explain below, is that as the games become more sophisticated and involving and the consoles more powerful, the consoles may be losing their appeal and may be soon thought of as "dinosaurs."

Are videogame consoles dinosaurs?

Molly Wood, a technology columnist for *The New York Times*, discusses the new consoles in an article titled "Two Game Consoles Battle for a Dubious Prize" (February 13, 2014, page B8). She writes:

> A philosophical war is being waged in the world of video game consoles.
>
> One view is represented by Microsoft's Xbox One: the console as home media hub, combining television, movie-watching, video streaming, games and computer like features such as Skype into a single device that's as much set-top box as gaming rig.

DOI: 10.1057/9781137565457.0013

A second view comes from Sony, whose PlayStation 4 is for playing video games first, for streaming video and watching DVDs second, and for little else.

Wood describes her experiences setting up the Xbox One in the article and concludes that it is extremely complicated while the PS4 was easy to set up and was "fun." But the real question, she asks, is whether video game consoles are out-of-date dinosaurs that will not be able to compete with game playing on tablets and phones. As she explains (February 13, 2014, page B8): "The real question, though, is whether the idea of a console itself is out of date." That is because, she adds, playing games on mobiles and tablets can be as immersive as on consoles and the games are much cheaper. It's hard to stomach paying $60 for games to be played on consoles when there are many inexpensive games for mobiles and tablets. Thus, she concludes, the PS4 may be better than the Xbox 1, "but in the end it may be a victory of one dinosaur over another."

That topic is discussed in a companion article on the same page of *The New York Times* in its Gadgetwise column, also written by Molly Wood. She points out that mobile gaming is becoming increasingly popular and that the iPad Mini and the Nexus 7 tablets are both very powerful and can run "graphically intense games in high-resolution." And there are many games that can be played on mobiles and powerful tablets and, now, computers. She mentions inexpensive alternative consoles, such as the $99 Ouyang that can stream Android games to television sets; there are around 500 games that have been created for the Ouyang, as well. On the basis of Wood's two articles, it would seem that video game consoles, such as digital cameras and many other devices, will eventually fall victim to smartphones and powerful tablets with very high resolution screens.

I checked on video games for mobiles and tablets on Google search and found sites such as "90 Best Free Android Games" "Monthly Top Mobile Games." One site, "10 Best Mobile Games for Hardcore Gamers" by Robert Workman (that appeared in Tom's Guide, August 30, 2013) discussed the development of mobile games:

> Most smartphone and tablet gamers spend hours playing casual fare like: "Dots" and any given version of "Angry Birds." However, the winds have begun to shift, with more developers working on hardcore games to sway console players onto mobile. Some conversions have fared better than others—Rock star's "Grand Theft Auto" and "Max Payne" games have both

DOI: 10.1057/9781137565457.0013

been well received—but there's a lot of great stuff out there you may have missed. From first-person shooters and racing titles to fighters and RPGs, here are 10 awesome mobile games that can deliver a console-like experience anywhere.

This would suggest that large numbers of videogame players will be migrating from consoles to mobiles and tablets.

Kinds of video games

An article by Steve Mullis, "Getting Back Into the Game: Finding the Right Game to Play" that appeared on March 30, 2014 in "All Tech Considered" offers an up-to-date classification of video games. He offers the following classes of video games and examples of each kind of Video game. The list that follows is based on his article and is my construction.

> **Action**
> Shooters: Call of Duty
> Fighters: Street Fighter II
> Platformers: Donkey King Country
> Action-Adventure: Metal Gear, Resident Evil
> **Role Playing**
> Massively Multiplying Online RPG (MMORG): *World of Warcraft*
> Action RPG: *Torchlight, Bastion*
> **Strategy**
> Turn-based: Civilization
> Real-Time: StarCraft 2, League of Legends
> Puzzle: Tetris, Minesweeper
> Simulations: Sims, Football manager
> Adventure (no subcategories)
> Myst, Gran Fandango
> Sports (no subcategories)
> Gran Turismo
> **Casual (no subcategories)**
> Candy crush

This classification system helps us make sense of the bewildering number and kinds of video games available. A hit video game that is available on only one platform can boost the sale of videogame consoles enormously, so there is a great deal of competition for great games.

DOI: 10.1057/9781137565457.0013

The Entertainment Software Association has a website: http://www.theesa.com/facts/pdfs/ESA_EF_2013.pdf that has a great deal of information about the video game industry. It has a different classification system for videogame genres (Table 6.1):

TABLE 6.1   *Kinds of video games*

Adventure	Strategy	Family
Sports	Arcade	Fighting
Shooters	Casual	Flight
Role playing	Children's	Racing

Note: Chart is my construction.

All the video classification systems differ in minor ways, but certain genres, such as casual games, puzzles and board games, and action/sports/strategy sell more than others.

This classification system doesn't tell us where a game such as *Virtual Valerie* belongs. In this game you are able to enter a beautiful woman's apartment and look through her purse, look at the books she's reading, and so on. In the game, you interact with Valerie, who, in one scene, is shown with a see-through brassiere and hose and is lying on the couch. She asks you to remove her brassiere that she says is too tight. The goal of the game is to remove all of Valerie's clothes and get her into bed with you. This game is an example of a number of erotic video games that are available to players. But many of the other genres feature beautiful women who are scantily dressed.

Statista offers some information on money spent, in dollars, on video games worldwide (found in Table 5.2, which is my construction).

TABLE 6.2   *Worldwide sales of video games*

Kind	2014	2015
Handheld	15 billion	16 billion
Mobile	17 billion	22 billion
Personal Computer	21 billion	21 billion
Video Game Consoles	49 billion	55 billion

Note: Chart is my construction.

I've seen other statistics that indicate that global consoles and games revenue will be around 46 billion US dollars in 2014 and an estimated

DOI: 10.1057/9781137565457.0013

41 billion US dollars in 2019, suggested a slump in the sales of consoles and games. We can see that the video game industry is an enormous one.

Video games can be played on special consoles designed for them, computers, tablets, and, increasingly, on smartphones. As I pointed out earlier, it looks like the smartphone will devastate, if not destroy, the videogame console industry, just as smartphones have destroyed the entry-level digital camera industry, but whether they actually succeed in doing so remains to be seen.

There are many sites on the Internet listing the best video games of 2013. I chose one from Top Tens, which is useful because it has descriptions of each game. The list follows (Table 6.3):

TABLE 6.3   *Top ten video games in the United States*

1.	Grand Theft Auto 5
2.	The Last of US
3.	Assassin's Creed 4: Black Flag
4.	Bioshock Infinite
5.	Minecraft
6.	FIFA 14
7.	Call of Duty: Ghosts
8.	Tomb Raider
9.	Batman: Arkaham Origins
10.	Battlefield 4

Source: http://www.thetoptens.com/best-games-releasing-2013/

In looking over sites with "best" videogames of 2013, I found that many of these games are found on a number of "best" game sites, but not always in the same order of popularity. The Entertainment Software Association has a website: http://www.theesa.com/facts/pdfs/ESA_EF_2013.pdf that has a great deal of information about the video game industry.

In 2015, a site on Forbes lists the top games of 2015 in alphabetical order: Assassin's Creed, Battlefeed Hardline, Batman: Arkham Knight, Below, Blood Forum, Dying Light, Evolve, Game of Thrones, Halo 5, Hotline Miami 2: Wrong Number and King's Quest. We can see that the list of games is quite different from the top ten list for 2013, which suggests that the popularity of different kinds of video games changes rapidly. http://www.forbes.com/sites/erikkain/2014/12/29/the-top-video-games-of-2015/

DOI: 10.1057/9781137565457.0013

Videogames, psyche, and society

Thanks to a Pew survey on gaming, we now have this information on the popularity of videogame playing in the United States:

> The report, titled Teens, Video Gaming and Civics is based on a national, random digit dial telephone survey of 1102 parent-teen pairs. The teens we interviewed were ages 12 to 17.
>
> Among the many findings of this study, we learned that gaming is nearly universal among teens, with 97% of American youth 12 to 17 playing computer, console, portable or cell phone games, and half of teens play on any given day, usually for about an hour. And…gaming isn't just the domain of boys—94% of teen girls play games, as do 99% of teen boys. Teens who play games span the racial, ethnic and socio-economic spectrum, in ways that young users of many other technologies do not. Gaming is also a social experience for most teens—76% of adolescents say they play with friends, either in person or online. As with the girls I watched, gaming is an integral part of the fabric of teens' social lives. Rather than keeping teens from interacting with peers (indeed, teens who game daily communicate and spend face to face time with friends just as frequently as teens who game less frequently), games often serve as a topic around which interaction is organized. Nearly a third of teens say they visit websites and online discussions about games they play.

We see that gaming is extremely popular with teens of both sexes and plays an important role in their social lives. One reason that video games play are so popular is that they are immersive and interactive.

Interactivity and immersion in video game

Janet Murray's book on video games, *Hamlet on the Holodeck: The Future of Narrative in Cyberspace* (1997) explains what interactivity in video games means: these games respond to our inputs and to what happens in a game. In essence, we are able to participate in the events that take place in the game and our participations affects the outcome of the game. Players of video games are faced with choices they must make at various times in a game and these choices help determine the way the game evolves and other choices that will have to be made. This is because of the branching structure of narrative video games. All possible choices and their outcomes have been programmed into the game, which means that the feeling players have that they are affecting the game is only

DOI: 10.1057/9781137565457.0013

an illusion. The creators of the games have already programmed in all possible choices and their outcomes.

These interactive video games can immerse players in simulated environments, offering them, at various times in the game alternative realities. Players have the same kind of experience that people do when they become engrossed in novels or plays or movies—that is, they become "lost" in the worlds that have been created for them or that, in the case of video games, they help create. This experience has been described by the English poet and critic Samuel Taylor Coleridge as "the willing suspension of disbelief" and involves our identifying with one or another characters in the story we are reading, seeing, or being told.

Video games provide what Murray calls "agency," which is a sense of satisfaction that players gain from making decisions and taking actions in playing the game—even though all actions have been programmed into the game. Video game creators face a problem, Murray suggest, in that the narratives they create must generate pleasure or "payoffs" for players at various places in the game who also derive pleasure from winning the game. They do this in three ways: through *immersion*, through *agency*, and through *transformation*. Different genres of video games enable players to transform themselves into many different roles, such as adventurers, space heroes, fighters, car thieves, and football players. As Murray explains:

> Storytelling can be a powerful agent of personal transformation. The right stories can open our hearts and change who we are. Digital narratives add another powerful element to this potential by offering us the opportunity to enact stories rather than to merely witness them. Enacted events have a transformative power that exceeds both narrated and conventionally dramatized events because we assimilate them as personal experiences. (1997: 170)

Being in immersive environments in which we play making decisions that matter—that is, having agency—is so powerful that certain video games are now being used, with some success, in psychotherapy.

There is, however, a negative aspect to immersive video games. The gratifications that video game players derive from being immersed in different worlds, from gaining a sense of agency, and from transforming themselves, if only temporarily into whatever they want to be are very powerful and, in many cases, playing video games is addictive for many people.

DOI: 10.1057/9781137565457.0013

Addiction and video game playing

An article by Robert W. Kubey, "Television Dependence, Diagnosis, and Prevention: With a Commentary on Video Games, Pornography and Media Education" offers some insights into the addictive nature of video games; a communication scholar, explains why video games are addictive (1996: 242):

> As with television, the games offer the player a kind of escape, and as with television, players learn quickly that they momentarily feel better when playing computer games; hence, a kind of psychological reinforcement develops. But video and computer games also have particular characteristics that make children and adults especially likely to report that they are "addicted" to them. There is the general challenge posed by the game and the wish to overcome it and succeed, and there is the critical characteristic that the games are designed to minutely increase in challenge and difficulty along with the increasing ability of the player.

What these games do, Kubey suggests, is offer cleverly calibrated and increasing but manageable levels of difficulty to players. They derive satisfaction from either solving the problems generate by the games or overcoming the difficulties that the games present. This means there is a subtle kind of reinforcement going on.

Kubey likens the experience of playing games to the work of psychologist Mihaly Csikszentmihalyi on "flow" experiences:

> Many of us are never quite as exhilarated as when we have harnessed our abilities and set them against a difficult but surmountable challenge. Video and computer games can offer children and adults such a challenge. Indeed...computer and video games offer all the essential features that we know are likely to result in a "flow" experience of intense and enjoyable involvement and a high level of concentration: closely matched skills and challenges in an activity and rapid feedback regarding one's performance. (pp. 242–243)

This helps explain why video games are so addictive; they are excellent in generating flow experiences.

There is another factor that helps explain video game addiction, what can be called the "escalation effect." Let me offer an analogy to drug abuse here. We know that as their bodies become accustomed to the drugs they are taking, drug addicts must keep increasing the dosage of the drugs they take to get the "high" they desire. Video game players may

DOI: 10.1057/9781137565457.0013

find themselves in the same kind of predicament: They need to spend more time playing games to obtain the level of pleasure to which they have become accustomed. Based on the discussion above, I think it is reasonable to suggest that there is an addictive aspect to video games.

Video games as cultural signifiers

A number of years ago, in 1984, when *Pac-Man* was popular, I wrote an article in which I interpreted what the game's popularity signified about American culture and society. My article appeared in *The Los Angeles Times* and led to any number of letters to the editor suggesting that I am out of my mind, a charlatan, and all wrong. Here is part of the essay (May 2, 1984):

> We can find in "Pac Man," I believe, a sign that a rather profound change was taking place in the American psyche. Earlier video games (and the video-game phenomenon is significant in its own right) such as "Space Invaders" and so on, involved rocket ships coursing through outer space, blasting aliens and hostile forces with ray guns, laser beams, and other weapons, and represented a very different orientation from "Pac Man." The games were highly phallic and they also expressed a sense of freedom and openness. ... "Pac Man," however, represents something quite different. The game takes place in a labyrinth which implies, metaphorically, that we are all trapped, closeted in a claustrophobic situation in which the nature of things is that we must either eat or be eaten.

I suggested, then, that this reflected a kind of regression that was taken place as we moved from games that were phallic in nature (with guns and rockets) to games that were oral in nature (with eating and biting) and that this regression was a means of young people, who played the game, dealing with a kind of diffuse anxiety from which they suffered. The great popularity of the game led me to suggest that it reflected psychological dynamics of considerable importance.

Readers of *The Los Angeles Times* weren't used to someone using psychoanalytic theory and semiotic theory to analyze a pop culture phenomenon, and a number of readers wrote rather nasty comments in their letters about my article. But this analysis of *Pac Man* suggests that popular culture, and in this case, video games, can be seen as indicators of trends taking place in a society that escape notice because they are so ubiquitous and seemingly innocuous and innocent. Except, that is, for games such as *Virtual Valerie*.

DOI: 10.1057/9781137565457.0013

7
Digital Watches and Smart Watches: *Everyone's Monitored*

Abstract: *This chapter, on digital watches and smart watches considers different attitudes toward time and discusses the writing of Mircea Eliade, who explained, in his book* The Sacred and the Profane, *that there are two different kinds of time: profane time, which passes and doesn't return, and sacred time, which is cyclical and sees past events as returning—as in some religious ceremonies. This is followed by six hypotheses on the meaning and cultural significance of digital watches, such as: they reflect the growth of alienation in contemporary societies and the triumph of the digital over the mechanical. The chapter concludes with a discussion of the various functions of smart watches and the creation of the Apple Watch.*

Berger, Arthur Asa. *Gizmos or: The Electronic Imperative: How Digital Devices have Transformed American Character and Culture.* New York: Palgrave Macmillan, 2015. DOI: 10.1057/9781137565457.0014.

Why do we call timepieces watches? The term "watch" has a suggestion of anxiety about something possibly menacing happening. Soldiers stand watch to guard their bases, and watching implies a need to survey one's environment to protect oneself against something dangerous. To watch is also connected with seeing: we watch a movie or a play. The term "timepiece" has different connotations and suggests that knowing and controlling time is what is crucial. Whatever we call them, timepieces or watches, they help us order our days and help us get to where we need to be on time—when we were supposed to be wherever we are going. And time that passes cannot be recovered. Or so we believe.

Mircea Eliade, a scholar of religion, explains that there are two kinds of time: profane time, which passes and disappears into some void, and sacred time, which is recoverable. He writes in his book *The Sacred and the Profane: The Nature of Religion* (1961: 70):

> Religious man lives in two kinds of time, of which the more important, sacred time, appears under the paradoxical aspect of a circular time, reversible and recoverable, a sort of eternal mythical present that is periodically reintegrated by means of rites. This attitude in regard to time suffices to distinguish religious from nonreligious man; the former refuses to live solely in what, in modern terms, is called the historical present; he attempts to regain a sacred time....Now, what is possible to observe in respect to a non-religious man is that he too experiences a certain discontinuity and heterogeneity of time. For him too there is the comparatively monotonous time of his work, and the time of celebrations and spectacles, in short, "festal time."

What we have to realize, Eliade points out, is that modern man and woman may think that they have escaped from sacred time and the sacred, in general, many of the things we do are camouflaged sacred rites and, to expand on this notion, there is a mythic component to many of the things we do, though we are not aware that this is the case.

Perspectives on time

In the Western world, our notion of time is that it is linear and passes. The present is a thin line between the past and the future that is constantly moving. Because time passes, it is precious to us, which explains why our watches are so important. Time is a valuable commodity that escapes us if we are not careful. It is always disappearing into the past. This is the profane world's understanding of time. But not everyone thinks that

DOI: 10.1057/9781137565457.0014

way. In his book *The Sacred and the Profane: The Nature of Religion,* Mircea Eliade explains the difference between profane time and sacred time (1961: 68–69):

> For religious man time too, like space, is neither homogenous nor continuous. On the one hand there are the intervals of sacred time, the time of festivals (by far the greater part of which are periodical); on the other there is profane time, ordinary temporal duration, in which acts without religious meaning have their setting....One essential difference between these two qualities of time strikes us immediately; *by its very nature sacred time is reversible* in the sense that, properly speaking, it is a *primordial mythical time made present.* Every religious festival, any liturgical time, represents the reactualization of a sacred event that took place in a mythical past, "in the beginning." Religious participation in a festival implies emerging from ordinary temporal duration and reintegration of the mythical time actualized by the festival itself. Hence sacred time is indefinitely recoverable, indefinitely repeatable. From one point of view it could be said that it does not "pass," that it does not constitute an irreversible duration.

The interesting thing is that most of us live in two times: profane time during our day-to-day activities, but sacred time during religious holidays and ceremonies, when we return to earlier times. A good example of this is the Jewish religious holiday of Passover. In the Bible God commands the Jews to celebrate Passover eternally and Jews relive, existentially, the escape of the Jewish forefathers from Egypt. This is done in the Passover Seder by Jews reading Haggadahs, which are books that are read and which list the order of actives to be followed out to celebrate the holiday.

So it is the case with religious people that although they live in profane time, and their watches help them structure their activities according to this time, they also, on occasion, live in sacred time as well. Sacred interludes occur quite regularly in many religions.

Hypotheses on the meaning of digital watches

In the 19th century, men carried pocket watches that usually had covers and would be kept in watch pockets on their vests. The pocket watch gave way to the wrist watch in the 1920s, which meant that women could wear watches, and the mechanical wrist watch gave way to the digital watch in the 1970s. The digital watch is dominant now, but a new kind of smartwatch, which not only tells the time but also enables us to read

DOI: 10.1057/9781137565457.0014

our email and can monitor various body functions has become popular in recent years. I'll have more to say about smartwatches later in this chapter.

In my book *Signs in Contemporary Culture: An Introduction to Semiotics*, I offer a semiotic analysis of digital watches from the 1980s, when my book was published. That is, I take the watches as "signs," the core concept in semiotics (which means the science of signs) and interpret what these watches reveal about society. I offer a number of hypotheses, which we can define as "guesses," about the significance of these gizmos. I offer these hypotheses with additional material about their "higher" meaning in contemporary American culture. Like so much in modern America, what I wrote about digital watches no longer has as much relevance, since many people no longer wear watches of any kind but rely, instead, on their smartphones This may be changing, since now, there are smart watches that often work in conjunction with smartphones that enable people to access their email, monitor their health, and do various other things. What I wrote about digital watches also applies to the new smart watches in many cases. I have modified my analyses and updated it in various places.

Digital watches reflect a growth of alienation in contemporary societies

The essence of the digital method is "finger counting" that translates, when we come to machines (such as clocks), to separate units. A digital watch flashes the time moment by moment, in contrast to the now "old fashioned" analog watch that is based on relationality. We tell the time on an analog watch by looking at the position of hands on a watch face. The digital watch is atomistic; it divides time into discrete parts, which flick by rapidly. The analog watch sees time as something unified and is rooted in history. Time passes but the cycle repeats itself every twelve hours, since most analog watches are based on a twelve-hour time frame.

The atomism and separation found in the digital watch leads me to suggest that societies where such watches are popular are more alienated than those in which analog (relational) watches are most popular. It may also be that individuals who wear digital watches are more alienated than those who do not. Alienation means "no connections" or no ties.

DOI: 10.1057/9781137565457.0014

"A" means no and "lien" means ties or connections. The development of watches that now monitor our bodies is the latest development in digital watches. They can connect our body functions to our doctors and to others, but they don't help us deal with the alienation in contemporary American culture and, in fact, turn our attention more toward ourselves and our bodies.

Digital watches reflect the triumph of the electronic over the mechanical in modern society

The traditional mechanical watches, with springs and winding mechanisms, are now old-fashioned "art objects" and do not have the power or resonance of the new electronic digital watches. Winding is a sign, generally, of the mechanical; in the electronic world one pushes buttons. There are, of course, some people who feel hostile to the new electronic order and who prize old-fashioned things such as mechanical watches and other relatively crude (though often beautiful) machines... What is important about all this is that the digital watch that helps us obtain a modern identity, gives us a "modern" look and feeling. The space-age modern style is becoming dominant in our culture. You can buy an excellent digital watch on Amazon.com for around ten dollars. An excellent analog watch generally costs much more and some mechanical watches cost hundreds of thousands of dollars.

People who wear digital watches have as greater sense of powerlessness than those who wear conventional analog watches

Digital watches are much more precise and accurate than analog watches, which means that we can be more careful about arriving at meetings on time and being where we are supposed to be when we are supposed to be there. And, God forbid, should we forget about an appointment, we can set an alarm on our watches to remind us that we have somewhere we have to be. You can set the watches to sound a short alarm every hour, which suggests a great concern for and consciousness about the passage of time. People who wear digital watches worry more about self-control than those who wear conventional watches.

DOI: 10.1057/9781137565457.0014

Digital watches enable their wearers to impose their concern about time upon others

If we set our watches to sound an alarm every hour, we make anyone who hears the alarm aware of the passage of time, which means that we are exercising a certain amount of control over those who hear our watches beeping on the hour. But even if we don't set our watches to beep on the hour, others who hear any watch beep become conscious of time and concerned about what the time is. Beeping watches are a problem in theaters and concert halls, though smartphones ringing are now a much more serious problem.

The dominance of the digital watch shows the power of fashion

Traditional mechanical watches, with springs and winding mechanisms, as I pointed out earlier, are now old-fashioned "art" objects and do not have the "I'm with-it" power or resonance of the new electronic digital watches. There are, of course, many people who do not like the new electronic order and prize old-fashioned things such as their mechanical watches and other, often beautiful, devices and gizmos. What digital watches do (or did, since they have now been replaced by the time-keeping apps on smartphones) is help us obtain a new identity, give us a more "modern" look. They reflect the power of fashion to shape our decisions about consumer products.

Digital watches are magical toys

There is something rather remarkable about these watches—they run silently, they are very busy with numbers appearing in rapid succession from nowhere—or so it seems. These watches seem to have a life of their own—a life that increasingly affects our lives and shapes our behavior. They are always bubbling with life and activity while we often have periods of rest and tranquility or activity (and sometimes exhaustion). They are in many respect magical toys. Our gadgets always have an aesthetic and functionality and we derive a great deal of pleasure from the beauty of these objects and their powers. The digital watch is a primitive device

DOI: 10.1057/9781137565457.0014

compared to smartphones, which have replaced digital watches for many people. Smartphones are the ultimate magical toy for children and adults.

The digital-watch phenomenon caught the Swiss napping

The Swiss underestimated the appeal of digital watches and discovered, to their chagrin, that shortly after the introduction of digital watches, that a major portion of their market had been stolen from them. That is because the Swiss watchmakers believed that beautiful machines would always be preferred over cheap space-age gadgets. This was an elitist conception that proved quite costly. The Swiss, of course, started manufacturing digital watches but they lost a large share of the market to companies in China and other countries. In recent years they have regained some of the market with their digital watches but the problem they face is that many young people don't wear watches but rely on their smartphones when they want to know what time it is.

The latest Gizmo we didn't know we needed: Smartwatches

Now, of course, digital watches are being superseded by smartwatches, though this innovation has just been introduced in recent years and is not popular yet with large numbers of people. But as more are sold and the price comes down, it is reasonable to assume that they will replace digital watches for large numbers of people. Samsung introduced a smart watch in February 2014, the Samsung Gear Fit, that is described below in one of their ads:

> Gear Fit is shaped like a wristband and has a 1.84-inch curved Super AMOLED screen with 432 × 128 resolution. That's enough room to easily show the time, date and exercise information. Why stop there, though? Gear Fit can also display incoming text messages, calls, email and data from apps such as Samsung's S Planner calendar app. Health data is tracked through a trio of sensors: an accelerometer, gyroscope and heart rate monitor.

So smartwatches can do a number of things and the Gear Fit competes with many health wrist bands that do monitoring but don't have the other

DOI: 10.1057/9781137565457.0014

capacities found in the Gear Fit. What we find is that smartphones and now, smartwatches, have the ability to do a number of different things, as reflected in the hundreds of thousands of apps for smartphones and the functions built into the new smart watches. We now are finding second-generation smart watches that have increased functionality, as in the Gear Fit, which has fitness functions, and better batteries, though the batteries are still a problem with these devices. The new Apple watch is expected to sell 19 million units or 56% of all smart watches in 2015. It looks like it will be yet another category killer for the Apple corporation, but whether Apple will sell huge numbers of these devices and make them "must buys" for people remains to be seen.

An article in the *Wall Street Journal Digits* offer some insights into one component of the digital watch business, so-called smart bands.

> According to the latest study by Canalys, this year's shipments of "smart bands"—devices worn around the wrist that can run apps just like smartphones—will likely *exceed* 8 million units. The research firm expects the fledgling market segment to triple to 23 million units next year and rise to 45 million units by 2017. The smart band category includes existing smart watches from **Samsung Electronics**, **Sony**, Pebble and others, but it excludes wristband-like devices that can't run apps. To put those numbers in context, **Apple** sold 51 million iPhones in the quarter ended December. 28.

Digital watches have come a long way since the early 1970s, when they first appeared. Some early digital watches only told the time when you pressed a button. I recall reading an article in a magazine that suggested the popularity of these early digital watches was connected to the feelings of power that owners of these watches had. Every time they pressed a button, they could summon time. Amazon.com has more than 2,700 fitness watches and many thousands of digital watches. In short, there are an enormous number of digital watches of all kinds available for people who wish to purchase one or more of them, including one for four dollars that monitors your heart rate and helps you count calories, among other things. We first encountered smartwatches in the comic strip, *Dick Tracy*. They were just a fantasy in the imagination of the strip's creator, Chester Gould, but now they have become a reality, and nobody knows how they will evolve, as our passion for wearable digital devices become more widespread and more intense.

There is reason to suspect that digital smart watches will become more popular now that Apple has introduced the Apple watch, which sells

DOI: 10.1057/9781137565457.0014

from \$350 to \$17,000. Tech writers who have used Apple smartwatches all say they are rather difficult to use but despite their flaws they are a valuable addition to the digital gizmo world. There is some question about whether this watch will catch on the way Apple's other products have and become category killers—that is, dominant in their field. The classical example of an Apple category killer is the iPhone.

Geoffrey A. Fowler describes the device in an article titled "The Hour of the Apple Watch Begins," which appeared in the April 9, 2015 issue of the *Wall Street Journal.* He writes (page D1):

> What's valuable is your time. The Apple Watch is a computer built to spend it better. And if you can tolerate single-day battery life, half-baked apps and inevitable obsolescence, you can now wear the future on your wrist...I only look at it in blips, for rarely more than five seconds. It shows me the weather with one finger swipe. It gets physical, gently tapping my wrist when something important needs my attention, and lighting up when I lift my arm to look. It nudges me when I've been sitting too long.

Like many digital gizmos, the Apple Watch and all its competitors will improve as time goes by. But I wonder whether I want a presence on my wrist that is so proactive, which seems to have a life of its own and which nudges me when it thinks I've not been active enough. The jury is still out on the Apple watch. It may be a digital device that we didn't know we needed until it was created and then we realized that we didn't need it.

DOI: 10.1057/9781137565457.0014

8

Digital Cameras and Photography: *Everyone's a Documentary Maker*

Abstract: *Digital cameras developed in 1975 and had an enormous impact and were very popular, but their very existence is now threatened by smartphones, such as the iPhone, which has a very good camera and has led many people to use their smartphones to take pictures rather than their digital cameras. I offer statistics that show that the sale of digital cameras dropped by 42% in 2014, with entry-level digital cameras suffering the biggest loss of popularity. Next I discuss the relationship between photographs and reality and the role photographs play in our image-centric world. This is followed by a discussion of a device, the narrative clip, that takes a photograph every thirty seconds and sends them to a computer for editing. I suggest that at the unconscious level, this device reflects an attempt we make to assert that our lives are important and have meaning. The chapter ends with a discussion of Google's Glass device.*

Berger, Arthur Asa. *Gizmos or: The Electronic Imperative: How Digital Devices have Transformed American Character and Culture.* New York: Palgrave Macmillan, 2015. DOI: 10.1057/9781137565457.0015.

DOI: 10.1057/9781137565457.0015

If you did any traveling to distant lands before the invention of the digital camera, you would find yourself lugging a rather heavy object that used expensive film. You had to be careful about your shots because you used up some of the film with each shot and you only got a certain number of shots with each roll of film. All that changed with the invention of the digital camera. With digital cameras you can take many photographs with no concern for using up precious film. That's because you can snap as many shots as you want and then, at your leisure, delete images you don't like, at no cost.

Digital cameras

Digital cameras developed around 1975 when Kodak developed a means of storing captured images digitally. How ironic is it that these cameras forced Kodak to stop manufacturing film and eventually become a minor player in the digital camera business. The problem the digital camera industry faces is that smartphones are developing better and better cameras and many people no longer bother taking their cameras on trips because they have their smartphones with them. In a *Wall Street Journal* article by Juro Osawa we find a discussion of a women abandoning a Canon DSLR camera for an iPhone, which enables her to post her images to Instagram and then to her many followers. The iPhone camera is very good but it has been surpassed by cameras in other smartphones in recent years.

An article from "Lies, Damn Lies and Statistics," a site with statistics on media (accessed March 5, 2014) explains the problems digital cameras face and offers some data on the number of photographs taken by people with cameras and smartphones:

> Last year, Japanese camera makers reported a 42% drop in global camera shipments, with sales of entry level digital cameras particularly badly hit. The cause was of course the proliferation of smartphones, and people using their mobile device as their main camera. The current evidence is that this trend is if anything accelerating. In July the *Wall Street Journal* reported that Japanese camera shipments had decreased by another 42% in the first five months of 2013. The WSJ article is behind a paywall, but it also includes reference to the no. of pictures taken every year...Fujifilm has estimated that 1.6 trillion photos are now taken annually with smartphones. That is far higher than the estimate Yahoo! provided earlier in the year, when it said that 880 billion pictures would be taken in 2014.

DOI: 10.1057/9781137565457.0015

This figure, of 1.6 trillion photos taken is, of course, just an estimate—but it points to the importance of the cameras in smartphones and the comment that it is the cameras that determine the choice of smartphones rather than the operating system that puts decision-making about the purchasing of smartphones in a different light. If it is possible to store an image digitally it is also possible to delete it or, in some cases and with some programs, manipulate it, which means that the photograph can no longer be used for documentary evidence.

Photography was born in 1826 when Nicephore Niepce took a picture of his garden with a device he invented. Over the years, photography became more and more important as an art form and record of reality until the digital camera arrived on the scene and demolished photography's place as a record of reality. Now, as smartphones have evolved, and the cameras in the smartphones have become better and better, digital cameras may be doomed to extinction. Smartphones have led to the sales of digital cameras plummeting. At first, it was only inexpensive, entry-level digital cameras that were affected but now sales of expensive digital cameras have fallen off as smartphones offer better and better cameras. Smartphones also allow "selfies," photographs that people take of themselves with the cameras on the front of digital cameras, and presidents and the Pope have been photographed taking "selfies" of themselves—generally with others. If the function of the photograph, for the most part, is to capture reality, the function of the "selfie" is to include oneself in the reality being captured. There may be an element of narcissism involved in "selfies" but it may be that "selfies" enable people to take photographs of themselves in various places instead of asking someone else to photograph them standing in front of some tourist spot of interest. A photograph of someone standing in front of the Taj Mahal or the Eiffel Tower of wherever is proof that one has been there.

Photographs and reality

Photographs, we now recognize, are not simple reflections of reality, as Howard Becker explains in his article "Aesthetics and Truth" (*Society*, July/August, 1980: 27):

> When people make or use photographs for scientific or scholarly purposes, they do not strive for unique visions or personal styles. Instead, they want material that helps them answer a question taken seriously in an established community

DOI: 10.1057/9781137565457.0015

concerned with such questions. Such photographs are frequently made in a standardized fashion, so accepted in the user community that its members think it is the only way such photographs can be made. But every choice embodied in those images—of framing, lens, lighting, printing—is a choice that could have been made differently, with a different photographic result.

What Becker points out is that photographs are not simple records of reality but interpretations of reality, for if you point your camera in a different direction or change the lighting or frame the shot differently, you get a different image.

We also have to consider what a person looking at a photograph knows, for that knowledge plays a role in the way we make sense of an image. As John Berger, a British novelist and writer put it, in *Ways of Seeing*, "The way we see things is affected by what we know or what we believe" (1972: 8). If you show a photograph of an airplane to people in an isolated village in Brazil, who have not had any contact with civilization, they would not know what it is. So, in a sense, we can say that what we know shapes, to a considerable degree, what we see or what we recognize in what we see.

Photographs also provide information to us about what is going on in some country where we don't have much information. Thus, China experts always studied the official Chinese May Day photographs to see who was in the photographs and who was left out or had been displaced. Photographs play a major role in social media sites such as Facebook, where approximately 75% of the entries have some kind of image in them: photographs of children, cats, dogs, places of interest, people, along with short videos, copies of articles, and that kind of thing.

The reason the camera is so important is that we now live in an image-centric world and thus photographs are the key elements in that world. The images we capture on our cameras (or, increasingly on our smartphone cameras) capture moments for us that often have emotional significance. With digital cameras (most of which can take videos) we can take as many photographs as we want without having any fear of running out of film or spending too much money. That means that the images we take are not precious; we can take so many images with our digital cameras that any given image isn't that important.

I can recall being on a boat in a river in India with a group of fellow tourists, who took what seemed like hundreds of photographs in the course of a couple of hours. The theory behind this kind of behavior is that with so many images, there probably will be a few that are memorable. The rest can easily be deleted with the press of a button.

DOI: 10.1057/9781137565457.0015

The Narrative Clip

The Narrative Clip is an interesting postage-stamp-sized camera that enables people to take five megapixel images every thirty seconds and send them to a computer where they can be organized into a narrative showing one's activities during the time the Narrative Clip was worn. As Elise Hsu explains in her piece, "Cool or Creepy? A Clip-on Camera Can Capture Every Moment," on the February 24, 2015 "All Tech Considered" on National Public Radio:

> Narrative's founder, a Swedish designer named Martin Kallstrom, says his wearable camera reacts to a real need: We don't often capture simple or seren-dipitous moments because we don't know they're significant until later. "What I wanted to achieve was to have a tool to make it possible for me to document stuff that I experience while I experienced them. Without taking me out of that moment," Kallstrom said. The always-on camera means being fully present, without pulling out a point-and-shoot. "You have special moments in your life where you want to be fully in that moment. Maybe spend time with your friends, or your kids," Kallstrom said.

The development of the Narrative Clip, described above, takes the power of cameras to record reality to new heights—or is it depths? The Clip takes photographs automatically every thirty seconds. That means it takes two photographs a minute, 120 photographs an hour, and if we leave it on for 16 hours, allowing 8 hours for sleep, it takes 1,920 photographs a day and 13,440 photographs a week, which we can then download to our computers and have a record of everyone we've met and everything we've seen.

It seems to be the opposite of the "selfie," but it actually is a kind of selfie, since it only captures images of what we see and places we go. What we get is what we might describe as a contextual selfie—images of all the people and things around us and part of our lives, but not ourselves. We remain invisible but we are there, in the background, as the Narrative Clip takes the photographs every thirty seconds. Narrative Clips reflect a diffuse obsession with recording everything in our lives, and they turn our lives into documentaries—except that the Clip doesn't edit the images it takes, though our computers have programs for doing that. Between the "Selfies" we take of ourselves and the Narrative Clip images that it takes, we have a comprehensive record of our lives. Before "Selfies," we relied on others to take photographs of ourselves. But the cameras on the screen sides of our smartphones have negated our dependence on others—except, that is, for long shots that focus on the places we are and not close-ups of ourselves

DOI: 10.1057/9781137565457.0015

with buildings in the background. As modern life becomes more and more alienating, the Narrative Clip is an attempt we make—not consciously, of course—to assert that the things we do and places we go matter and have meaning. A narrative is a story. The term "narrative" comes from the Latin *narratus* that means "to make known." Narratives have a linear dimension and a structure. According to Aristotle, who was one of the most important theorists of narratives, they must have a beginning, middle and an end and they serve to instruct us and have an emotional impact. The Narratives from the Narrative Clip are like serial music—they just keep on going, repeating themselves and never leading to a conclusion. The Clip takes images based on the wearer's activities, but doesn't rearrange them; it merely records one's activities and functions as a visual record of the wearer's meetings with others and activities. It is not a work of art but a random collection of images based on the activities of the wearer of the Clip, though presumably we can edit the images in our computers. It seems to me that the Narrative Clip is a kind of journal in the form of images and has something in common with video games that don't have avatars in which we react to our surroundings and challenges that come our way, but are never seen. Life becomes a video game just as video games are now becoming more real than life. When one watches the images as they have been recorded by the Narrative Clip, one's life takes on the character of a slide show or a person playing a video game such as Myst.

Google Glass

The Google Glass, a high-tech pair of glasses that have a video camera embedded in it, is the next step beyond the Narrative Clip. The Narrative Clip snaps photos every thirty seconds of whatever it sees, but that is relatively primitive when compared to the Google Glass that can take videos whenever the person wearing the Google Glass wants to do so. The Google Glass turns everyone wearing this device into videographers and can turn every experience the wearer has into material for making a personal documentary. An article in *The Guardian* by Michael Rosenblum deals with the revolutionary potential of this remarkable device. He writes:

> Google Glass is the first in what is sure to be a long list of wearable computers—things that are going to change the world just as surely as the printing press did...it is a small, fairly unobtrusive eyepiece that you wear like a pair of

DOI: 10.1057/9781137565457.0015

glasses, which allows you to see the web, and to be online, all the time. It may be called wearable, but I prefer to think of it as embeddable—that is, you are effectively and personally "embedded" in the web all the time. Glass gives the wearer not only the ability to access information and content at anytime, anywhere in the world, it also gives them the ability to capture, create and put their own content into the web all the time.

http://www.theguardian.com/media-network/michaels-rosenblog/2014/mar/07/google-glass-technology-changing-world.

Because the Google Glass can make videos unobtrusively, many people see it as an infringement on their privacy and wearers of the Google Glass are not permitted to wear the device in some bars and other places. There is a question of whether it is legal to wear the device while driving. With this device, we become, in a curious way, a content receiver and content provider, all at the same time.

Google Glass came to an untimely end on January 19, 2015 when Google stopped making it available to people who wished to purchase it. Critics have suggested that it wasn't launched correctly, it looked "goofy" on people, and that it created problems with its front-facing camera, possibly violating people's privacy. In August 2015 we find that Google Glass has risen from the dead and a new version, aimed at the workplace, is being released, with a consumer version scheduled for a year later. An article by Alistair Barr in the July 31, 2015 issue of the *Wall Street Journal* (page B4) discusses the new version of Google Glass, which has an improved battery, a faster processor, and improved wireless connectivity. Barr suggests that the new workplace version might be used by surgeons to get advice from colleagues or field workers who need instructions on how to repair machinery. Unlike Apple, which creates products we didn't know we needed, the Google Glass seems to be a product that was created and has been redesigned for people, in certain fields such as medicine, and so on, who didn't need it but now might find a use for it. Whether consumers will be interested in the new version remains to be seen, for unless Google can figure out what to do about the way Google Glass invades our privacy, it is hard to see why people will want to purchase them.

DOI: 10.1057/9781137565457.0015

9
Computer Printers:
Everyone's a Publisher

Abstract: *This chapter deals with the way that the price of computer printers has declined rapidly as their functionality has increased. I suggest that the new computer printers make everyone who owns them potential publishers and the existence of inexpensive print-on-demand publishers, such as Amazon.com's Create Space, allows people with these printers to actually become publishers. I offer an example of my publishing a little book I wrote on English character and culture. The chapter concludes with a discussion of a new printing technology, 3-D printing, also called "additive manufacturing," which has revolutionary potentials in everything from manufacturing to medicine.*

Berger, Arthur Asa. *Gizmos or: The Electronic Imperative: How Digital Devices have Transformed American Character and Culture.* New York: Palgrave Macmillan, 2015.
DOI: 10.1057/9781137565457.0016.

Over the course of many years, I've purchased a number of computers and many different kinds and brands of printers. And every year the cost of these printers has dropped, considerably. The printer I have now is a Brother HL-2140 laser printer that cost something like 60 dollars. My wife has the same model, as well. I decided to buy a laser printer because I got tired of continually having to order ink cartridges for the inkjet printers I had. My printer is a monochrome printer, but it is possible to buy color laser printers for around 130 dollars, at the low end, at Amazon.com. There are many other color laser printers for around 200 dollars and up. Wireless color inkjets costs around eighty dollars and up, depending upon what features one wants. Below I offer a Timeline for the evolution of the printer based on an article in Wikipedia.

1976—Dot matrix printer.... is a type of computer printing that uses a print head that runs back and forth, or in an up and down motion, on the page and prints by impact, striking an ink-soaked cloth ribbon against the paper, much like the print mechanism on a typewriter. However, unlike a typewriter or daisy wheel printer, letters are drawn out of a dot matrix, and thus, varied fonts and arbitrary graphics can be produced.

1969—Laser printing is a digital printing process that rapidly produces high quality text and graphics on plain paper. As with digital photocopiers and multifunction printers (MFPs), laser printers employ a xerographic printing process, but differ from analog photocopiers in that the image is produced by the direct scanning of a laser beam across the printer's photoreceptor.

1976—Inkjet printing....is a type of computer printing that creates a digital image by propelling droplets of ink onto paper. Inkjet printers are the most commonly used type of printer, and range from small inexpensive consumer models to very large professional machines that can cost tens of thousands of dollars.

1986—3-D printing is a process of making a three-dimensional solid object of virtually any shape from a digital model. 3-D printing is achieved using an *additive process*, where successive layers of material are laid down in different shapes. 3-D printing is considered distinct from traditional machining techniques, which mostly rely on the removal of material by methods such as cutting or drilling (*subtractive* processes).

DOI: 10.1057/9781137565457.0016

Information from Wikipedia.com

My first printer was a dot-matrix device, and though it seems really primitive now, it was an amazing breakthrough when it first came out, because it meant that I could reproduce images as well as letters. From dot-matrix printers I moved on to inkjet printers, which I used until ten years ago. They are excellent devices but not good for people who do a lot of printing, since they were always running out of ink. My final move was to a laser printer. It uses an ink cartridge that can print several thousand pages.

What has happened is that computer printers are now commodities and have gone down in price a great deal over the years. I remember paying 400 dollars for a laser printer not too many years ago. Now, I have a better laser printer that cost only 60 dollars and the cost of printing a page has dropped a great deal as well.

In 1970, when I moved to Mill Valley (where I still live) I joined a small press club. It was made up of hobbyists who had small presses, with which they printed various things. It takes a lot of work to set type and once you've set the type and printed something, you have to distribute the type back in the special drawer that printers use. Type also costs money so most hobby printers don't have very many type faces. As soon as computers started becoming popular and computer printers became inexpensive, the small press club lost its reason for being. There are still some former members who have their printing presses and drawers full of different type faces, but most members decided "why bother, when I have a hundred typefaces I can use on my computer and I can print things so easily with my computer printers."

What the computer printer means is that everyone is potentially a publisher, if it is possible to print out a book-length manuscript, formatted to look like a book, and have it duplicated at a print center. What you get is a fairly primitive book, stapled together. I did this twenty years ago before the development of print-on-demand devices. I sent the book to a publisher and it ended up being published as *Signs in Contemporary Culture: An Introduction to Semiotics*, after I added some material.

With the development of print-on-demand presses, one can have a book published by one of the many Internet publishers, for relatively little money. I recently published a book, *A Year Amongst the UK: Character and Culture in England in 1974*, using Amazon.com's Create Space publishing service for around $2.35 a copy. It is full of my drawings

DOI: 10.1057/9781137565457.0016

and other images. That's what it cost me to purchase a book from Create Space. Authors can sell their books for whatever they want. Create Space doesn't charge anything to set the book up; they only charge for each book ordered—plus mailing. Create Space makes its money as a printer and, if people want technical help, by providing artists and book designers. As a result of the development of these print-on-demand presses, the number of people self-publishing books has skyrocketed and something like 200,000 self-published books come out each year now. Traditional publishers publish around 100,000 books a year. In 2010, around 330,000 new books and editions were published and around 200,000 of them were self-published.

When I taught, I found that my students seemed to pay more attention to the typography and look of their term papers than they did to the content of their papers. What I found, often, was that although the papers looked beautiful—the students often inserted colored images and the typefaces they used were fine, the papers were full of spelling errors, awkward passages, and unclear sentences. The students were so involved with their printers that they neglected the papers they had written.

The latest technological change in printers is the development of 3-D printers—printers that use a coil of some kind to build things. An article in Wikipedia explains how these printers work.

> **3D printing** or **Additive manufacturing** is a process of making a three-dimensional solid object of virtually any shape from a digital model. 3D printing is achieved using an *additive process*, where successive layers of material are laid down in different shapes. The 3D printing is also considered distinct from traditional machining techniques, which mostly rely on the removal of material by methods such as cutting or drilling (*subtractive* processes). A 3D printer is a limited type of industrial robot that is capable of carrying out an additive process under computer control. While 3D printing technology has been around since the 1980s, it was not until the early 2010s that the printers became widely available commercially. The first working 3D printer was created in 1984 by Chuck Hull of 3D Systems Corp. Since the start of the 21st century there has been a large growth in the sales of these machines, and their price has dropped substantially. According to Wohlers Associates, a consultancy, the market for 3D printers and services was worth $2.2 billion worldwide in 2012, up 29% from 2011.

These printers run from basic 3-D printers, which cost around 400 dollars to many thousands of dollars, depending upon the capacity of the printer.

DOI: 10.1057/9781137565457.0016

There is a problem created by these devices. It is now possible to use a 3-D printer to make a plastic gun that can shoot bullets. Since these guns are plastic, they can get by screeners at airports which means terrorists, armed with such guns, could possibly take over an airplane. Although this sounds bizarre, law enforcement experts are worried about the power of these printers. They have also been used to duplicate credit card monitoring devices and steal money from ATMS.

There are now 3-D printing companies, with huge, industrial-sized printers, that can print objects based on designs sent to it by people employing these companies. People can email designs to the printing company and it uses one of its industrial strength 3-D printers to make the object. Because these printers are so inexpensive, they are used by chair designers to build chairs, by doctors to make body parts, and by all kinds of other people for an almost infinite variety of uses.

DOI: 10.1057/9781137565457.0016

10
Flatbed Computer Scanners: *Everyone's an Art Director*

Abstract: *In this chapter I explain that scanners turn everyone with a computer into a potential art director, for scanners allow us to scan images we like and save them in various programs such as Picasa. We live in an image-centered society, which explains why 70% of the content on Facebook is images. I offer an example of how having a scanner with optical character recognition allowed me to publish a manuscript I wrote in 1973. I also discuss the use of my scanner in publishing images on postings on Facebook and other sites. Finally, I discuss the development of a new art form—scanner art, in which artists use their scanners to create pastiches, some of them elaborate and imaginative works of art.*

Berger, Arthur Asa. *Gizmos or: The Electronic Imperative: How Digital Devices have Transformed American Character and Culture.* New York: Palgrave Macmillan, 2015.
DOI: 10.1057/9781137565457.0017.

Flatbed computer scanners are handy devices. They convert photographs, written material, printed material and objects into digital files, which can then be manipulated in various ways by computers. At Amazon.com they sell hundreds of different computer scanners, ranging in price from around 30 dollars to many hundreds of dollars, for high-powered scanners that have automatic feeders and are designed for commercial use. I have a Canon LiDE 200 scanner, which cost around 80 dollars when I purchased it a number of years ago. It still costs that much now. It is possible to get multifunction scanners that also are fax machines, but these devices don't scan as well as single-purpose scanners.

People who need to scan large numbers of documents—to save them electronically rather than in banks of filing cabinets can purchase high-speed sheeted scanners, which cost considerably more than the traditional flatbed scanner. For example, Brother has a sheeted scanner that costs $736. It can scan one-sided documents at twenty-four pages a minute and two-sided documents at forty-eight pages a minute. Fujitsu has one for $854 that scans in color. These sheeted high-speed scanners allow people to scan large numbers of documents very quickly and are standard items now in many "paperless" offices. They also allow users to find scanned documents electronically, which is much faster than trying to find them in a filing cabinet.

Scanners turn people into art directors

What scanners do is turn anyone with a computer into an art director. You can scan photos and other images into your computer and then manipulate the images with any one of a number of free programs. You can then use these images for many different purposes. I use my scanner to scan drawings I've made to use to illustrate my books. I send the images to my publishers to use in books that I'm publishing with them and I also use the images for self-published books. You can also use scanners to make copies of documents, which you can then email to people.

There are now what we might describe as scanner artists, who use scanners to create artistic images that they see as works of art. Thus, Christian Staebler writes:

> Scannography (also called scanography, Scanner Photography or Scan- art) is a new way to represent the world around us...Scannography is near from photography but also very different from it in many points. A few of them

DOI: 10.1057/9781137565457.0017

are the absence of perspective and of depth of field, the regularity of the light captured by thousands of captors...Some of these points are very different from one artist to the other. The material seems to have its importance too. One of the most interesting things about scannography is that it is a new way to see the things around us. It's not macro but can be! It's not drawing but has something similar to those documentary drawings done to capture the essence of plants or animals! It's not photography but it reproduces the reality with extraordinary precision! The term is subject to discussions, I chose the "scannography" with two "n" because I thought it suited with the fact that most scannographers do a real graphic work based on scanner (with two "n") captured images. Scannography is also the term for medical scans but that shouldn't be a contrariety. Some artist prefer "scanography" with one "n" as "scan" is ended with one only. In the early days of photography it wasn't considered at all as an Art. It's up to us to make scannography seen as something special that has its place in Fine Arts...

infos [@] scannography.org

Whether the works created by scanner artists are "real" art is something that will be decided over the years, but there is no question that some of the images created by scanner artists are quite beautiful.

Scanners in schools

Many schools now make use of scanners and other digital devices in courses in which students are asked to create illustrated narratives about their families (or some other topic of interest to them) or some other topic their teacher assigns them. Dealing with images has a particular power to engage students who are making these narratives and help them develop a beginning sense of visual literacy. We live in an ocular-centric world and the digital camera (and now the smartphone) and the scanner play a major role in our visual culture. In essence what students do when they make the illustrated narratives in their courses is make primitive documentaries, except their medium tends to be the PowerPoint presentation, though many schools have video cameras that students can use and many students have smart phones with video-making capabilities. For example, if students are making a story about their families, they may not only take photos of their parents and siblings but also scan old photographs of their grandparents, great-grandparents, and other family members.

DOI: 10.1057/9781137565457.0017

As Jason Ohler explains in his article "The World of Digital Storytelling":

> Digital storytelling enters the academic mainstream, the technique shows great promise. Creating digital story taps skills and talents—in art, media production, storytelling, project development, and so on—that might otherwise lie dormant within many students but that will serve them well in school, at work, and in expressing themselves personally. In addition, digital stories develop a number of digital, oral, and written literacies in an integrated fashion. This technique takes advantage of the fact that students are comfortable with narratives and attracted to digital enhancements that sharpen their critical thinking, research, and writing skills. Through creating narratives, students develop the power of their own voices and become heroes of their own learning stories. Most important, digital storytelling helps students become active participants rather than passive consumers in a society saturated with media.
>
> http://imoberg.com/files/World_of_Digital_Storytelling_The_Ohler_J._.pdf

Images are important because you can show your readers or audiences things you want them to see (such as photos of people or places you've visited in your travels) rather than trying to describe these things with words. So scanners play an important role in communication, and can be used to illustrate letters and make flyers, and postings on social media as well as being used for scanning images for books.

A National Council of Teachers of English Advice Sheet about scanners, found on the Internet, offers the following suggestions for how they may be used in the classroom:

> Scan in photographs relevant to school projects.
>
> Scan in pupils' drawings for use in presentations and on school Web sites.
>
> Young children can scan their hands at the beginning and end of the school year to measure growth. Students with special needs can scan in pages from a book or document and use scan/read software to have it read aloud.
>
> Electronic versions of documents, reports, school administration data and forms can be produced. Scanning of images from a variety of sources for slide shows in subject areas.
>
> http://www.ncte.ie/documents/advicesheets/11ScannersNov08.pdf

We see, then, that scanners can be used in many ways in schools, and not only in art or media departments.

If you look at Facebook you see that the postings generally contain visual images. I have a blog on Facebook, "Arthur Asa Berger and the Literary Life," on which I write about my literary activities and

DOI: 10.1057/9781137565457.0017

adventures and also post various drawings I've made and photographs I've taken. Lately I've taken to scanning illustrations I've made for my books and posting them on my blog. I found thirty illustrations from my book *Signs in Contemporary Culture: An Introduction to Semiotics* and scanned the illustrations, with the text on the page on which they appear in my book, and saved them in Picasa. Then I made a file with the illustrations and put it on my desktop. Now I put the illustrations, one a day, onto the blog. Below I offer an example of one of my scans (Figure 10.1).

This does two things: first, it enables me to show my "followers" (few but dedicated) one of my images and second, it saves the trouble of having to write something new each day for my blog. So the scanner enables me to function like an art director at an advertising agency and find images for various purposes. I did the same thing with drawings I've made of famous cultural theorists such as Roland Barthes, the French semiotician, and thinkers such as Sigmund Freud and Karl Marx (Figures 10.1 and 10.2).

I would describe scanners as essential tools for anyone with a computer and a printer. Let me offer an example of how useful scanners can be (Figure 10.4).

In 1974, I spent a year in England and while I was there I wrote a little book about my adventures and about English character and culture. I called in *A Year Amongst the UK*. A woman who lived next door to our house in London was a typist and I hired her to type up the book. When we returned to America, I put her typed version of my book in a filing cabinet and promptly forgot about it. I didn't think conventional publishers would be interested in it and I couldn't use it in its typed form. Then I discovered optical character recognition and was able to use OCR with my scanner to turn the typed version of my book into a word document. That, in turn, enabled me to publish it with Create Space, Amazon.com's self-publishing company. The book is a slender volume of 108 pages and each copy costs me around $2.30 to print. I illustrated it with drawings and photographs I had and published it to give to friends as a gift (Figure 10.5).

Some people probably think of scanners as unnecessary but I would argue just the opposite. If you don't have a scanner, there are many things you can't do because you lack the ability to capture images and textual material, which you can then manipulate on your computer. When you have a scanner you become an art director and can use it for

DOI: 10.1057/9781137565457.0017

Definition 5

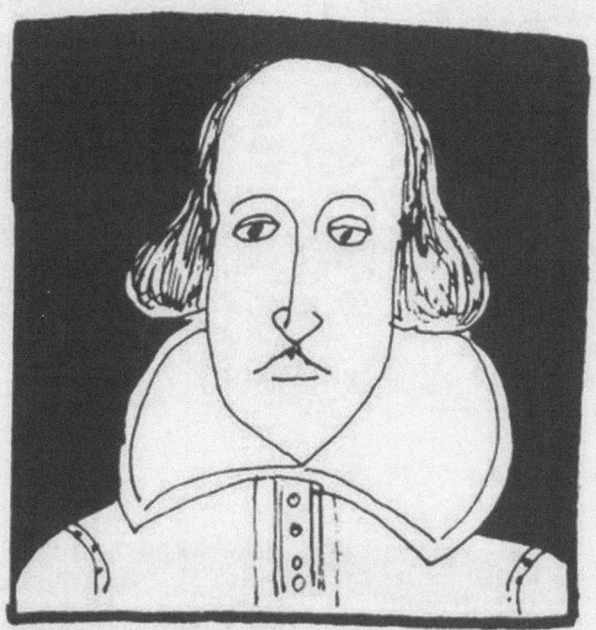

In this application we concern ourselves with one of the most important kinds of signs—words, and, in particular, the word "honor." Is "honor" just a word? And is a word just "air," as Falstaff argues?

HAL AND FALSTAFF AND THE PROBLEM OF HONOR

One of the more interesting aspects of Shakespeare's *Henry IV, Part 1* is the way in which honor is handled. The play deals with a number of topics and has a number of themes: the education of a king, Hal's search for a father, his calculating and cold intelligence, and so on, but of chief interest here is the matter of how honor is treated. Shakespeare may not have read any of the semiologists, but he certainly understood the subject.

When the play opens, Hal's father, the king, is bemoaning the "fact" that his son is a wastrel, and is comparing Hal to Hotspur, Northumberland's son. The King says, discussing Hotspur's triumphs on the battlefield:

Yes, there thou makest me sad, and makest me sin
In envy that my Lord Northumberland

FIGURE 10.1   *Scan from* signs in contemporary culture

DOI: 10.1057/9781137565457.0017

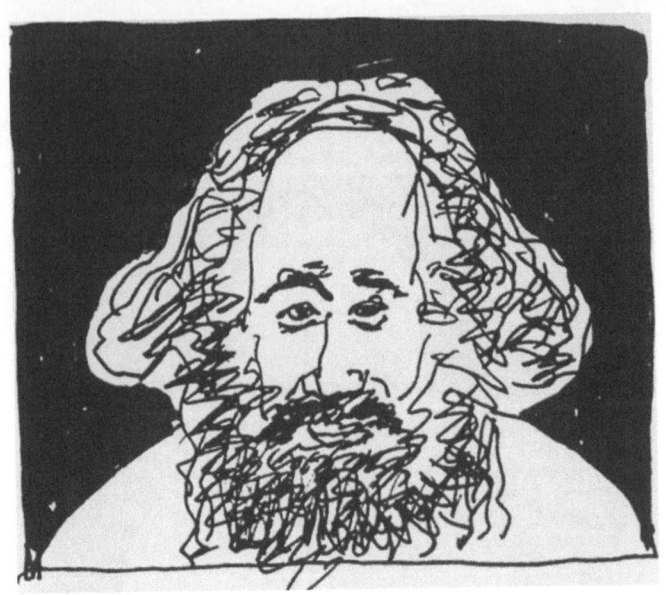

FIGURE 10.2   *Karl Marx*

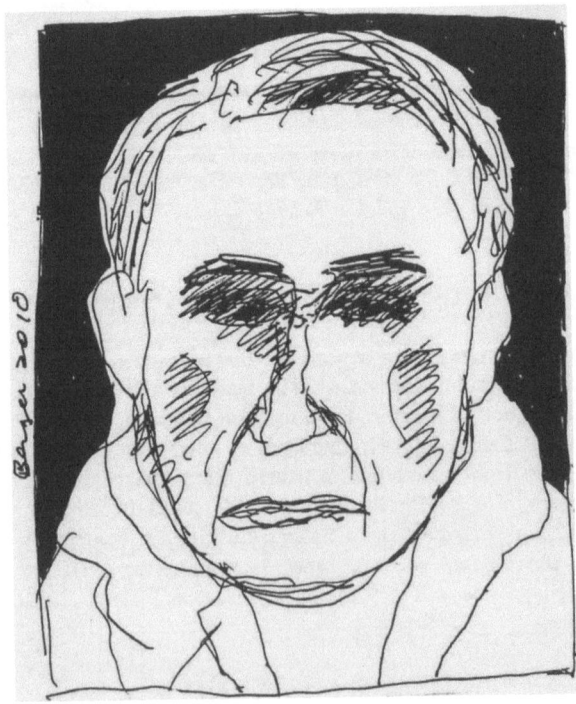

FIGURE 10.3   *Roland Barthes*

DOI: 10.1057/9781137565457.0017

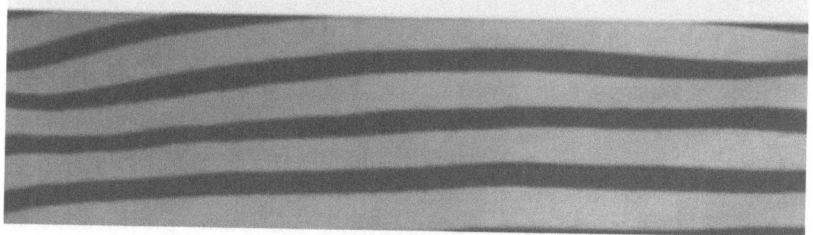

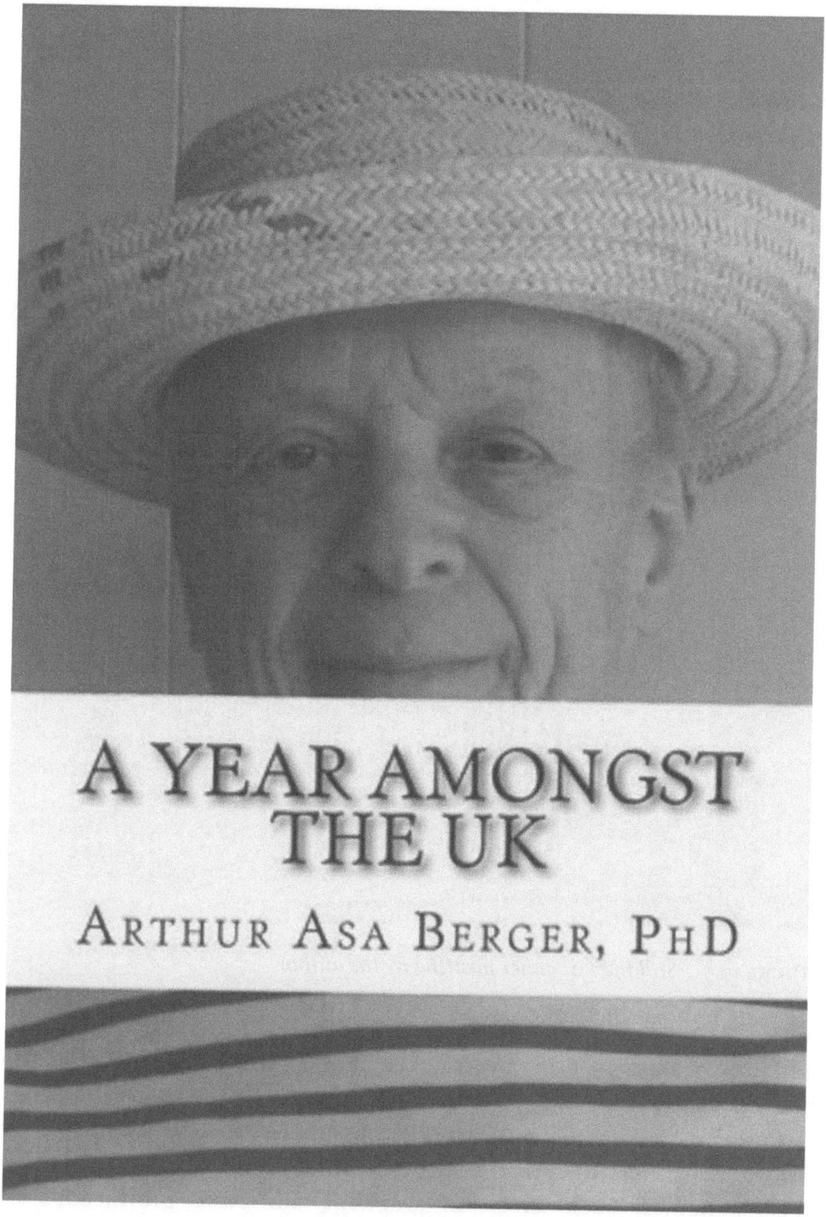

FIGURE 10.4   *Cover of book on English character and culture*

DOI: 10.1057/9781137565457.0017

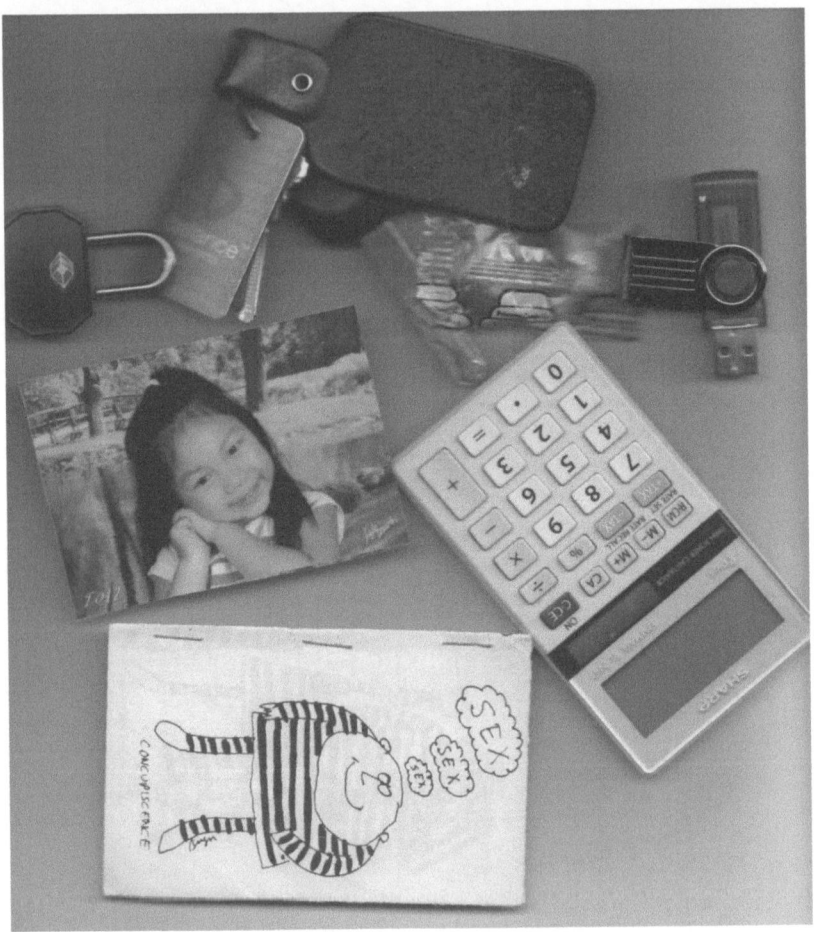

FIGURE 10.5   *Still life 1: scanner pastiche by the author*

all kinds of things—things you never thought you could do before you had a scanner.

And you can also become an artist, for there are now scanner artists who use scanners to create works of scanner art. They call themselves various names, such as scannographers, and have produced some remarkable images/works of art—similar in nature to pastiches, the classic postmodern art form—except that they use objects placed on a scanner instead of tearing up pieces of paper with different things on them and gluing them to a piece of cardboard or stretched canvas on a

DOI: 10.1057/9781137565457.0017

frame. You can find the works of scanner artists if you Google "scanner art." As Christian Staebler points out in the quote at the beginning of this chapter, scanners provide a "new way to see things around us."

What we learn from the analysis of digital flatbed scanners is that our electronic gizmos are incredible enablers and that people who purchase these devices find all kinds of different ways to use them. Used in conjunction with digital cameras and computers, they play a major role in providing the images that pervade our social media.

DOI: 10.1057/9781137565457.0017

Coda

This book has been a wild adventure for me because when I set out to write it I didn't know what I would find. I suspected that our digital devices had interesting secrets to reveal to me but I wasn't sure what I'd discover or whether I could even find enough material to write a book. When I analyze a text, like an advertisement, or interpret the meaning of an object, like a camera, I use certain techniques I have mastered—such as semiotics, psychoanalytic theory, and Marxist ideological theory, and I am often surprised by what they yield. Some scholars, not sympathetic to qualitative analysis and the kind of writing I do, might suggest that *Gizmos* is mostly fantasy and that I use quotations from scholars to suggest that I am serious. That is, what I "find" in the gizmos I analyze is in my mind and not in the Gizmos. Once, when I was lecturing on Americana culture and society and giving a reading from my book *Bloom's Morning* in Vietnam, someone in the audience asked me if the book was a novel—so I may be writing fiction in this book without realizing it.

Gizmos happens to be the fifth book I've written on material culture, though I've been writing articles about material culture for many years. In 1964, when I was a graduate student in American Studies at the University of Minnesota, I happened to pass by a new McDonald's restaurant that opened. It had gigantic arches and a sign that kept flashing incredible numbers, indicating the number of people who had purchased a hamburger from McDonald's. The arches suggested religion to me; the sign indicated the size of the "congregation," and the price of

DOI: 10.1057/9781137565457.0018

the hamburger was so small I saw it as being like a donation. So I wrote an article for *The Minnesota Daily* titled "The Evangelical Hamburger," in which I argued that McDonald's was similar, in some respects, to evangelical religions. It caused a big stir in Minneapolis. So you see, I tend to see things in terms of other things, to see the world analogically (metaphorically) and I combine this imaginative perspective with documentation from writers and scholars of all kinds whose work, I believe, gives us something to think about and help make my ideas creditable.

There's no end to what engineers and scientists will be bringing our way. Lately it is "wearables" and perhaps someday soon "implants." There is widespread fear now, as reflected in books such as Eric Brynjoflsson and Andrew McCabe's *The Second Machine Age*, that intelligent robots (with digital brains) will be replacing many of us—lawyers, stock traders, doctors, nurses, professors, ad infinitum, and we won't have the kinds of jobs we used to have or the lifestyles to which we have become accustomed. There's also a considerable amount of anxiety about the possibility of new technologies "going wrong" and causing havoc, at the least, and creating computers, machines, or intelligent robots that possibly will enslave us or even end up killing us.

The digital devices I have analyzed in this book can do remarkable things for us, and, so we've discovered, to us. The question I asked at the beginning of this remains to be answered—who will be master? Some would say the real question is "how long will we remain master?"

DOI: 10.1057/9781137565457.0018

References

3-D Printing or Additive Manufacturing. Wikipedia.

Ante, Spencer. 2013. "Smartphone Upgrades Slow as the 'Wow' Factor Fades." *The Wall Street Journal*, July 17, page B1.

Baudrillard, Jean. 1996. *The System of Objects*. London: Verso.

Becker, Howard. 1980. "Aesthetics and Truth." *Society*, July/August, page 27.

Berger, Arthur Asa. 1984. "Pac Man." *The Los Angeles Times* May 2.

Berger, John. 1972. *Ways of Seeing*. London: British Broadcasting System "British Spies Said to Intercept Yahoo Webcam Images." *The New York Times*, February 27, 2014.

Dichter, Ernest. 2002. *The Strategy of Desire*. New Brunswick, NJ: Transaction.

Dreyfus, Hubert L. 2008. *On the Internet*. New York: Routledge.

Editorial on Smartphones and police surveillance. 2014. *The New York Times*, April 28.

Eliade, Mircea. 1961. *The Sacred and the Profane: The Nature of Religion*. New York: Harper & Row.

eMarketer, "US Teen Smartphone Users Versus Tablet Users", 2012–2013.

eMarketer, "Attitudes Toward Mobile Devices According to US Millennial Smartphone Users", June 2014.

Erikson, Erik. 1963. *Childhood and Society*. New York: W.W. Norton.

DOI: 10.1057/9781137565457.0019

Esslin, Martin. 1982. *The Age of Television*. San Francisco: W.H. Freeman.

Fowler, Geoffrey A. 2015. "The Hour of the Apple Watch Begins." *The Wall Street Journal*, April 2, page D1.

Gartner. July 2015. www.gartner.com. Hardy, Quentin. 2014. Hardy, Quentin. 2014. "Smartphones, The Disappointing Miracle." *The New York Times*, March 2.

Kubey, Robert W. 1996. "Television Dependence, Diagnosis and Prevention: With a Commentary on Video Games, Pornography and Media Education," in Tanis M. Macbeth (ed.), *Tuning in to Young Viewers: Social Science Perspective on Television*. Thousand Oaks, CA: Sage Publication.

Levy, Steven. 2010. "How the Tablet Will Change the World." *Wired*, March 22.

Lunenfeld, Peter. 1999. *The Digital Dialectic: New Essays on New Media*. Cambridge, MA: The MIT Press.

Mariani, John. Pew Internet Newsletter.

Mullis, Steve. 2014. "Getting Back Into the Game: Finding the Right Game to Play," on *All Tech Considered*, March 30.

Murray, Janet. 1997. *Hamlet on the Holodeck: The Future of Narrative in Cyberspace*. Cambridge, MA: The MIT Press.

Patai, Raphael. 1972. *Myth and Modern Man*. Englewood Cliffs, NJ: Prentice-Hall.

Schechner, Sam. "Web Enabled Toothbrushes Join the Internet of Things." *The Wall Street Journal*. http://online.wsj.com/news/articles/S B10001424052702304360704579415161522531046

"Smartphones." www.pcmag.com

Steinberg S.R. and J.L. Kincheloe. (Eds) 1997. *Kinder-Culture: The Corporate Construction of Childhood*, Westview Press, 104.

Wood, Molly. 2014. "Two Game Consoles Battle for a Dubious Prize." *The New York Times*, February 13.

Workman, Robert. 2013. "10 Best Mobile Games for Hardcore Gamers." *Tom's Guide* (Internet site), August 30.

Zaltman, Gerald. 2003. *How Customers Think: Essential Insights into the Mind of the Market*. Boston, MA.

DOI: 10.1057/9781137565457.0019

Index

"90 Best Free Android
     Games," 67
"10 Best Mobile Games for
     Hardcore Gamers," 67
"7 Deadly Sins: Where
     Hollywood is Wrong About
     the Future of TV," 46

"Aesthetics and Truth," 86
Age of Television, 39
Amazon.com, 91, 93
*Amusing Ourselves to Death:
     Public Discourse in the Age
     of Show Business*, 38
Andreesen, Marc, 16
Annenberg School of
     Communication, 40
Ante, Spencer A., 34
Apple, 33–34
     "1984" television
        commercial, 60
     6 Plus iPhone, 298
     iPhone, 25
     laptop, 2
     mini iPad, 2
     story of Adam and Eve and
        Apple icon, 60
     versus IBM in "1984"
        commercial, 60
     watch, 82–83
ARPA: Advanced Research
     Projects Agency, 12
Atanasoff, John Vincent, 15
Auletta, Ken, 47

Babbage, Charles, 15
Baudrillard, Jean, 1, 5
Becker, Howard, 86–87
Berger, John, 87
Berners-Lee, Tim, 16
Bezos, Jeff, 16
Bloom's Morning, 106
Boluk, Liam, 46
Brooks, David, 32
Brynjoflsson, Eric, 107

Cambridge University, 13
Canon LiDE 200 scanner, 97
Clark, Jim, 16
coda, 106–107
CNET, 18
Commodore 64, 59
computers, 58–64
     chart with statistics on sales
        of, 63
     facial scanning, 63–64
     single comprehensive global
        library and, 59
     Vibralimage facial
        recognition program,
        63–64
Consumer Electronics
     Association, 47
Consumer Reports, 29
"Cool or Creepy? A Clip-on
     Camera Can Capture
     Every Moment," 88
Create Space, 91, 93
Csikszentmihalyi, Mihaly, 73

DOI: 10.1057/9781137565457.0020

Dichter, Ernest, 1, 6
Dick Tracy, 82
digital
    binary nature of, 8
    defined, 8
digital cameras, 84–90
    battle vs. smartphones, 85
    decline in sales of, 85–86
    Narrative Clip camera, 88
    photographs are interpretations of
        reality, 87
    "Selfies" and, 88
digital devices
    cameras, 84–90
    computers, 58–64
    digital watches, 75–83
    electronic imperative and, 3
    printers, 91–95
    scanners, 96–1056
    smartphones, 25–35
    tablet computers, 49–57
    television sets, 36–48
    our attachment to, 9
    use of term "gizmos," 6
    video game consoles, 65–754
    what they reflect about American
        culture, 3
digital watches
    as magic toys, 80–81
    caught Swiss napping, 81
    and growth of alienation in modern
        societies, 78–79
    hypotheses on meaning of, 77–78
    imposing concern about time on
        others, 80
    and power of fashion, 80
    sacred and profane time, 76
    sense of powerlessness in
        wearers, 79
    and smart watches, 75–83
    smart watches which we didn't know
        we needed, 81
    tablet computers, 49–57
    television sets, 36–48
    triumph of electronic over
        mechanical, 79

Doctoroff, Tom, 39
Dreyfus, Hubert L., 11, 17, 20

Economic Times, 66
Eliade, Mircea, 55, 75–77
Entertainment Software Association,
    69–70
Erikson, Erik, 25, 31
Esslin, Martin, 39–40
Evangelical Hamburger, 107

Facebook, 17
Facebook blog, "Arthur Asa
    Berger and the Literary Life,"
    99–100
Forbes, 70
"For Millennials: The End of the TV
    Viewing Party," 47
Fowler, Geoffrey A., 83
Freud, Sigmund, 4, 57

Gerbner, George, 40
"Getting Back into the Game:
    Finding the Right Game
    to Play," 68
Gizmos
    as material culture, 6
    used for gadgets, 6
    who is in control?, 8, 107
Goel, Vindu, 18
"The Good Wife," 40
Google, 19, 33, 34, 105
Google Glass
    death and rebirth, 90
    described, 89
    relation to Narrative Clip, 89
    wearable or embeddable?, 90
Google Nexus 4, 12
Gould, Chester, 82
Guardian, 89

*Hamlet on the Holodeck: The Future of
    Narrative in
    Cyberspace*, 59, 71
Hardy, Quentin, 26
Her, 9

How Customers Think: Essential Insights into the Mind of the Market, 4, 57
"How the Tablet Will Change the World," 51
Hsu, Elise, 88
HTC, 33
Hull, Chuck, 94

ink jet printer, 93
internet, 10–24
    and addiction, 21
    dictionary definition of, 14
    and electronic imperative, 13
    everyone is connected, 10
    issues with, 17–18
    loneliness and isolation, 20–21
    negative impact on society, 11
    of things, 22–23
    positive impact on society, 11
    problem of bullying and, 19–20
    problem of privacy, 18–19
    timeline, 15–16
iPad, 50–51, 56
iPad minis, 51–52
iPhone, 26, 34

Jobs, Steve, 50, 57
Johannsen, Scarlet, 9
Journal of Affective Disorders, 21

Kindle, 2
Kopstein, Joshua, 64
Kubey, Robert W., 73

Levy, Steven, 49, 51
LG, 33
"Lies, Damn Lies and Statistics," 85
Los Angeles Times, 74
Lunenfeld, Peter, 1, 8, 62

Macintosh "1984" television commercial, 59–61
Mariani, John, 23
Marxist ideological theory, 106
material culture, 6

McCabe, Andrew, 107
McDonald's, 106–107
"The Mentalist," 40
Microsoft, 49, 66
    power point program, 62
    Xbox, 66
Minnesota Daily, 107
"Monthly Top Mobile Games," 67
Moses, 52, 54–56
Motorola, 33
Mullis, Steve, 68
Murray, Janet H., 59, 71–72
Myst, 89
Myth and Modern Man, 55
myth
    chart, 56
    defined, 55
    model explained, 55

Narrative Clip
    description of, 88
    nature of narratives, 89
    relation to "Selfie," 88
    turning our lives into documentaries, 88
National Council of Teachers of English, 99
National Science Foundation, 64
National Security Agency NSA, 18
Net Smart: How to Thrive Online, 11
New Yorker, 47, 63
New York Times, 18, 26, 32, 47, 66–67
Nexus 7, 52
Nielsen Reports
    digital devices, 2
    everyday lives and digital devices, 2
Niepce, Nicephore, 86

Obama, Barack, 32
OCR: Optical Character Recognition, 100
Oedipus Complex, 6
Olympics, 36, 42–43
On the Internet, 11, 20
"Outside the Box: Netflix and the Future of Television," 47

DOI: 10.1057/9781137565457.0020

Pac-Man, 74
Patai, Raphael, 55
PC Magazine Encyclopedia, 26
Penroth, Nicole, 18
Pew Internet Newsletter, 23
Pew Research Internet Project, 23
Picasa, 96
Postman, Neil, 38
printers, 91–95,
   3D printing or additive
      manufacturing, 95
   evolution of, 92
   laser, 93
Provenzo, Eugene, 66
psychoanalytic theory, 106
   consciousness and unconscious, 3–4
   iceberg as representation of psyche, 4
   unconscious imperatives and
      behavior, 4
   Zaltman on 95-5 split in psyche, 4
Putin, Vladimir, 43

Rheingold, Howard, 11, 17
Rosenblum, Michael, 89

*Sacred and the Profane: The Nature of
   Religion*, 75–76
Samsung, 33–34
Samsung Google Chrome, 62
San Francisco Chronicle, 37
scanners, 96–105
   defined, 97
   scannography, 97–98
   turn people into art directors, 97
   use in schools, 98–99
Schechner, Sam, 22
*Signs in Contemporary Culture: An
   Introduction to Semiotics*, 78, 93, 100
Simon Personal Computer, 26t
smartphones, 25–35
   and alienation in Capitalist
      societies, 34
   description of, 26
   Erik Erikson on use by adolescents,
      31
   Freudian view on, 29

functionality of, 32
Marxist views on, 29
primary way to access internet, 28
statistics about, 28
"Smartphones, The Disappointing
   Miracle," 26
Snowden, Edward J., 18, 61
"Sochi's Other Legacy," 64
Society, 86
Sony, 66
Sony PlayStation, 66
Space Invaders, 66
Staebler, Christian, 97, 105
Strategy of Desire, 6
Super Bowl, 40
System of Objects, 5–6

tablet computers, 49–57
   defined, 50
   myth model and, 52–57
   and phablets, 56–57
   and unconscious, 57
   two questions about, 51–52
television, 36–48
   amount of time spent viewing, 38
   important role in consumer culture, 39
   kinds of sets and prices chart, 37
   The Media Book, 39
   medium full of dramas, 39–42
   medium we love to hate, 38–39
   Olympics, 40
   Over-the-top OTT, 46
   reliance on sports, 44–45
   statistics on viewing, 45
   Super Bowl and advertising, 41
   "Television Dependence,
      Diagnosis, and Prevention:
      With a Commentary on Video
      Games," 73
Tomlinson, Ray, 15
Torah: the Five Books of Moses, 55
"Two Game Consoles Battle for a
   Dubious Prize," 66

"Video Game and the Emergence of
   Interactive Video," 66

DOI: 10.1057/9781137565457.0020

video games, 65–74
  addiction problem and, 73–74
  agency and, 72
  are consoles dinosaurs?, 66–67
  as cultural signifiers, 74
  and flow experiences, 73–74
  interactivity and immersion,
    71–72
  kinds of games chart, 68–69
  popularity in United States, 71
  top ten video games in US
    chart, 70
  transformation and, 72
Virtual Valerie, 69, 74
worldwide sales of chart, 69

Wall Street Journal, 34, 83, 85, 90
*What Objects Mean: An Introduction to
  Material Culture*, 35
WiiU video game console, 66
Wikipedia, 50
Williams, Alex, 47
Wired, 51
Wood, Molly, 66–67
Woolf, Virginia, 13, 32
  "The World of Digital Storytelling," 99
Workman, Robert, 67
  *Year Amongst the UK: Character and
    Culture in England in 1974*, 93, 100

Zaltman, Gerald, 4, 57

DOI: 10.1057/9781137565457.0020